D0482194

MEMOS FOR MANAGEMENT

Leadership

MEMOS FOR MANAGEMENT

Leadership

JAMES L. HAYES

amacom

American Management Associations

This book is available at special discount
when ordered in bulk quantities. For information,
contact AMACOM, Special Sales Department,
135 West 50 Street, New York, NY 10020.

The articles in this book were previously published
in the following periodicals:

Management News *(January 1970–November 1974)*,
© American Management Association, Inc.

Managers' Forum *(December 1974–April 1977)*,
© AMACOM, a division of American Management
Associations.

Management Review *(May 1977–June 1982)*,
© AMACOM, a division of American Management
Associations.

Library of Congress Cataloging in Publication Data

Hayes, James L.
  Memos for management.

    1. Management—Addresses, essays, lectures.
I. Title. II. Title: Leadership.
HD31.H379   1983   658   82-73521
ISBN 0-8144-5767-3

First Printing

To Polly

Acknowledgments

One of my tasks as president of the American Management Associations was to write a column each month for our membership magazine, *Management Review*. Our membership included (and still includes) managers at all levels, from all types of organizations, from both the public and private sectors, and from both for-profit and not-for-profit organizations. This diversity challenged me into addressing a wide range of issues in my columns. I tried to exchange ideas with presidents one month, with first-line supervisors the next month, and then with both line and staff people another month. On the other hand, the diversity of our readership proved to be an extremely valuable resource as well, because all kinds of managers from all kinds of organizations contributed ideas and suggestions. I am grateful to each of them.

The fine people at all levels who worked with me at the American Management Associations taught me a great deal as well. Many passages of my columns reflect their dedication, their wisdom, and their values—and no acknowledgment would be complete without a tribute to their participation with me in many successful undertakings.

More specifically, I owe much to Jack Roach, Tommie Rendero, and the other AMACOM editors who have helped me over the years. They kept me consistent, readable, and on time. Ernie Miller, group vice president of publications, was always generous with his time as I posed philosophical or technical publishing problems. Rob Kaplan, editor-in-chief of the AMACOM book division, was very helpful in preparing this material for publication in its present form.

Finally, to a host of practicing managers who shared their aspirations and frustrations, and to a group of academic friends who speculated on a better management world in all fields, my thanks.

James L. Hayes

Contents

Foreword

What is man, that thou art mindful of him?

For thou hast made him a little lower than the angels, and hast
crowned him with glory and honor.

Psalms 8:4-5

The need to provide a foreword for a book is not readily obvious
except in the rare instance of a very young man or woman who has
made an important contribution, where a few words of recommen-
dation by a leading figure in the field may do no harm. This hardly
applies in the present case. Nor have I been asked to write a eulogy:
Jim Hayes is allergic to any kind of pomposity, however well meant,
and would loathe it.

I have known Jim Hayes for many years. I've worked with him,
served on his board, counseled him, been counseled by him, and
been with him on good days and on bad days. So I'm no neutral
observer, no impartial critic. Long ago, I developed a boundless
admiration for him and read many of these essays in their original
form. In rereading them, though, I have to confess, my experience
was like having the author in my living room, softly playing

études—little studies—on the piano, with wise though calloused and unsuspicious fingers.

Frankly, I haven't enjoyed a collection of essays so much since reading Lewis Thomas's *The Lives of a Cell*. In fact, as I reflect on these two books, I have come to the conclusion that they are uncommonly remarkable and have a lot in common, not the least being their short, readable chapters, perfect for those tiny chunks of time which we—too miserly—consign to personal growth. What they share, these two men and their books, is a lifetime devoted to understanding how living, breathing systems—that is, people and organizations—work, and how they can be nurtured and developed. Their wisdom is contained in that opening quote from the Psalms: that we are all "lower than the angels" yet at the same time capable of "glory and honor."

There are two fundamental ideas that inspire and inform every page of this book, and the thought and action of Jim Hayes. First is the conviction that management, in view of its great influence in the contemporary world, ought to have a code of ethics and a system of objectives going beyond the purely economic sphere (which, in any case, it has long overlapped). Second is the conviction that present-day mass civilization, more dynamic and richer in technical and scientific resources than in any period in the past, should make every effort to achieve the "kingdom of vocations," a human society organized so that all people may give their best by expressing themselves most fully and constructively.

This is exactly what Jim Hayes does in this book, with profound simplicity.

Warren Bennis

PART ONE

Leadership

1 People: The Reason and the Key

An effective organization is a living thing: An organization *is* its people. People breathe life and purpose and energy into an organization. An organization has a manner, spirit, tempo, nature, character. It has moods, joys, fears, and sorrows. But most important of all, an effective organization has a purpose that is shared by all its members and to which they willingly commit their efforts. People working together can do almost anything.

STRUCTURE AND EFFECTIVENESS

Some managers have suggested that the form or structure of an organization determines its effectiveness. Form and structure do bear on effectiveness just as the form and structure of a person will affect his or her ability to run or ski or climb a mountain. Form and structure are like bones and muscles; they set limits. But a person's spirit determines the meaning and reality of these limits; only those who press the limits know their reality—and few do.

So, too, for an organization: Its form and structure may set limits on its ability to perform, but only well-motivated people can make a reality of those limits—and rarely does this occur. Differences in performance, therefore, are not so often a matter of how an organization is put together as they are of how well a company succeeds in bringing the motivated application of the talents of its people to bear on its problems.

Differences in effectiveness are not attributable, you see, to resolving such problems as the roles of line and staff or to drawing handsome organization charts or to applying matrix organization structures to the activities of an enterprise. None of these techniques will work if the people who make them work do not care about or recognize the importance of personal, intelligent, goal-directed cooperation. It is such human aspects of organized effort that determine its effectiveness.

Obviously, theories of organization, systems of management such as management by objectives, and many other such techniques have been developed by practical men to help solve organizational problems. However, techniques developed for one set of circumstances and for problems of one nature are too often inappropriately generalized for application to completely different circumstances or to problems with markedly different structures. The value of techniques as general aides to problem solving is oversold—often by well-meaning people. But the result is no less unfortunate.

FINE IN THEORY BUT . . .

In the organizational context, we have all seen how organizational techniques that are fine in theory can produce unfortunate results in practice. Take the concept of profit centers. There is no question that this can be and usually is an effective, sensible way to organize. But is it sensible and effective when it is coupled with a managerial reward system that penalizes managers in charge of profit centers if they cooperate with their associates for the good of the entire organization? Here structure and its correlated system hinder the fully effective functioning of the human system by making cooperation less rewarding than competition.

Organization structure can also produce a *we* versus *them* attitude among employees and thereby reduce overall organizational effectiveness. Think of the problems with headquarters staff groups and outlying divisions. There is almost an intrinsic we/they situation in this pattern of organization. Who among us hasn't experienced the wall of resistance erected by those in one or another of these enclaves when we have tried to enter from the outside? So here again is an example of organizational form impeding organizational functioning—even though the form in theory *should* function well.

Job descriptions, another tool of organizational planning and human resources management, often hurt organizational effectiveness more than they help, particularly if they are not presented properly to an organization's members. How many times have you heard employees say, "But that's not my responsibility; it's not in my job description."

Broad Accountabilities, Not Tasks

Such reactions to as useful an administrative tool as job descriptions are unfortunate. Management must be at fault if employees view their job descriptions as tight and mutually exclusive definitions of job duties and responsibilities rather than as broad statements of job accountability that are to be applied by intelligent collaboraters striving to reach the organization's overall goals. If this broader attitude can be instilled, job descriptions become not restrictive definitions of jurisdiction but charters of accountability. Remember, too, all job descriptions have the same first item: Help the team.

And what one individual is totally responsible for any result? Certainly some individuals will have played a more important part in accomplishing some goal than will have others. But in an organizatonal setting, no one person can be completely responsible for any result. Too many people who came before him helped prepare the way; too many people who worked beside him carried a part of the load. Implicitly, and of necessity, all effort is team effort, all results team results. Any organization structure or management technique that suggests otherwise is unrealistic and inhibits the very cooperation and teamwork needed for effectiveness.

Other management techniques may also reduce the effectiveness of the human organization. Think of the highly detailed long- and short-term plans some organizations create that so inhibit flexibility and creativity. Think of the compulsive computers that spew out reams of paper reporting data that managers too often don't have the time to review much less to understand. (But who these days can slow down the computer?) And think too of the PERT charts and CPM networks with their chilling determinism. How many of you have felt your pulse quicken and your heart race at the sight of a PERT chart? Useful? Yes. Inspiring to the human side of the organization? Only to the very few who admire such elegance.

THE REASON AND THE KEY

It is not hard to see that some of us have lost our way as we have tended to emphasize the mechanical and systematic nature of management over the human and emotional. Perhaps my view is somewhat distorted, but I think that everything an organization does both within and outside begins and ends with people. In the most fundamental sense, I believe that organizations exist to serve people and that only in the sense of serving people through organizations do people serve organizations.

People are the reason and the key. There is little doubt that as the reason, people can be difficult, perverse, stress provoking, unreasonable. But what would be our purpose without them?

As the key—that is, as those who contribute to organizational effectiveness and human satisfaction—people might respond better if we managers began again to emphasize the old-fashioned virtues of understanding, patience, charity, selflessness, compassion, generosity. These virtues are addressed to the needs of the human organization—of people—and it is cooperating people who are effective.   [1977]

2   Top Management: A Job for a Team?

"We believe no one person can effectively manage a business our size or, indeed, most of our stores." These words were part of an announcement of a "changing of the guard" at the May Department Store Company. The announcement described the firm's "tandem principle" of management—also known, more broadly, as the co-manager concept. This kind of structure is based on the idea that, as Peter Drucker put it, "top-management work is work for a team rather than for one man."

The practice of having a "team" of top managers has been part of the business world for well over 50 years. In nonbusiness areas of management it is even more basic: in large religious organizations it has been used for centuries; it is built into the structure of the armed forces; and hospitals have been trying for decades to reconcile the medical staff with the administrative staff in terms of decision making.

Yet the concept of a top-management team *has* had its skeptics and detractors. Corporate officer and organization expert Alvin Brown, writing in the 1940s, expressed a belief that was commonly held at that time: "It is to be doubted . . . whether a principal can, consistent with effective administration, share with another principal the power to require performance." The "unity of command" principle was so popular—in fact, fundamental—in those days that when a top executive found his job too massive he employed the services of an "assistant-to" rather than share responsibility.

Even though the assistant-to position can be a valuable time-saver, however, it comes with its own problems. As Ralph Cordiner of General Electric, quoted in *Business Week*, declared, "It is our firm belief that such titles or positions create confusion as to responsibility, authority, and accountability, and tend to retard the growth of the company."

Beyond these considerations, the functions and responsibilities of today's leader are different from what they were years ago; and as a result, the sharing of power is beginning to look more attractive. Among the functions of the leader, two seem to be dominant today: the achievement of the purposes and objectives of the organization and the achievement of harmony both within and outside the organization. The first of these requires a hard drive toward favorable bottom lines, larger markets, and greater productivity and efficiency. The second requires sensitivity to people-problems, a tolerance for the time development takes, and a real concern for social responsibility. The trend toward sharing of top authority suggests that the capabilities for discharging these two major functions may not often be found in one person.

The result is specialization. In some organizations, authority is shared by two top executives designated "chief executive officer" and "chief operational officer." We also find such titles as "chief administrative officer" and "chief fiscal officer." The resurrection of the "office of the president" (meaning more than one person) and the expanded use of the executive committee constitute more evidence of the change taking place.

In developing a top-management team, two elements are significant: the compatibility of the participants and the ability of the organization to respond to multiple leadership.

Complete trust must exist within the team. Open identification of the strengths and weaknesses of each member of the team is fundamental, since tasks must be assigned to the particular person best equipped to handle them. Overlap is inevitable and must be accepted. Patterns of succession must be kept flexible, and politicking within the group would be lethal. Information flow must become far less formal, going beyond the "need to know." Controls and information need a uniform base, and there should be a central facilitator (usually the chief executive officer) to keep channels of communication open.

Members of some organizations are finding it difficult to adjust to this type of top structure—particularly if they have been accustomed to a strong central administration. "Who's running the company?" they wonder uneasily. Orientation of managers below the top levels is imperative, as is a careful explanation of the various career opportunities a team structure provides.

More and more organizations will be switching to co-management structures as the demands on the top office intensify. Many canny executives believe that this form of participation is not only demanded by growth; it is a basic condition of *intelligent* growth.   [1975]

3   The Entrepreneurship Recession

A British management leader, in a recent article, observes that American management has crested and cites our prolonged recession as evidence. It is unfortunate that the quality of management is so often equated with the immediate profit picture, because management is not exclusively related to profit. The test of management's strength goes far beyond immediate profit—to the long-term well-being and vigor of society.

Perhaps what our British friend has witnessed is not the result of any cresting of American management concepts but rather a decline in entrepreneurship. Strong professional management can ensure order and sober thinking, and even provide the vehicle with which to ride out a recession. But entrepreneurship is needed if we are to continue forging ahead.

Good management and entrepreneurship are not synonymous. Many management principles seem like the things that entrepreneurs do instinctively. The major difference is that what the entrepreneur does he usually does alone—and success today usually requires a combination of numerous talents. The entrepreneur cannot be described as a professional. He often is a "loner" with a highly centralized organization. He is impatient with time, extremely confident of his own talent, and respectfully skeptical of what is known. Many entrepreneurs have lost a fortune or two in a lifetime. Some have died rich, some in poverty.

But we can't discount entrepreneurship. The entrepreneur adds vision to his planning, flexibility and uniqueness to his organization, instinct to control, and above all, daring to decision making. When that rare individual—the entrepreneur with professional management talent—evolves, history is made, be it in the public or private sector.

9

ENTREPRENEURSHIP STIFLED

Promoting the climate for the development of entrepreneurs is difficult. Unsound thinking can stifle them or drive them out of the organization. Decentralization and delegation are the food on which entrepreneurship thrives. Heavy controls designed to let everyone know what everyone else is doing create a fishbowl effect and suppress risk taking. The dominance of the financial-accounting syndrome can be deadly. The future is not really significant if earnings per share or a line-item budget are overriding considerations.

Because management can never abdicate its right and responsibility to control the organization, some of the procedures that inhibit entrepreneurship are necessary. But policies and procedures governing every turn will restrict the growth of managerial judgment and kill off entrepreneurship. Endless meetings, sloppy communications, and red tape steal the entrepreneur's time.

GOVERNMENT BARRIERS

Even government, in pursuing the best of purposes, erects great barriers for the entrepreneur. It will not thwart great entrepreneurs, but it prevents new ones from showing through fast enough. Government agencies have many good managers but very few entrepreneurs. It is very difficult for the average government servant to account for a dream, risk a failure, or regulate the unknown. The entrepreneur finds it difficult to be heard out when he must account to those who represent the entire public. Space exploration, the SST, and military research had been notable by exception—but within the past two years, the nonentrepreneurial group has stopped "this foolishness." This is not to debate the rearrangement of priorities, but to indicate the inability of government to foster or sustain entrepreneurship.

COMPANY NEEDS

Many companies today are extremely conscious of their need for good management people and have excellent programs for hiring and developing them. Often what they get in return are young managers who are very demanding about high starting salaries—and can get them, work a standard day religiously, keep in line, and concern themselves about security. The effect is that the company may have many good managers, but no entrepreneurs. This may work for today, but tomorrow's result may be the kind of recession that will be much more difficult to pull out of than the present one.

[1972]

4 *Jīngshen*

Jīngshen is the Mandarin word for spirit and vivacity. It is an important word for all who would lead, because above all things, spirit and vivacity set effective organizations apart from those that will decline and die. And leaders by their words and actions build or kill an organization's spirit.

It is too easy these days to explain an organization's success in terms of its material wealth or its capital goods or the quality of its science, as if things and knowledge get things done. Things and knowledge are inert, inanimate, passive. They lie dormant until applied by people. Just as a violin's sound depends on the skill and personality of the violinist, so does the usefulness of things and ideas depend on the skill and spirit of those who use them.

By recognizing that spirited people make the difference, we have not really advanced the management art. Down through the ages leaders have known that the spirit of their troopers, seamen, farmers, teachers, scientists to a great extent determined the outcome of the struggle. And long ago, too, it was found that, while mercenaries would fight well for money and plunder, and slaves would fight well from fear and for freedom, free men would fight hardest and longest, and against any odds, to save their freedom and to accomplish the goals to which they had freely committed themselves. This lesson is still relevant today.

BOSSES FAIL

But even today there are bosses—to call them leaders would demean the term—who rule by fear. These are the drivers who march *behind* their people with the whips of firing or loss of opportunity in their hands. These are the managers who say, "Stop coddling Mary, she's lucky to have a job." Or, "Harry, you're not showing the attitude that people must have to advance here."

Bosses *do* create attitudes in their workers, but they are not attitudes that lead to productivity. The attitudes they create don't lead to harmony, they lead to fear and discord—and sabotage. When whipped, people will run or fight. If they run, they will run in any direction, not necessarily the direction in which the organization wants them to run. If they fight, they will fight using fair means and foul, and people fighting with their supervisors—and among themselves—obviously are not working for the common good.

The days when an organization could buy people's commitment are also past. The fear of loss of income is much less today than in the past. With national social welfare programs developed to the extent they are, few people face starvation if they become unemployed. Nevertheless, some managers view money as the only sound motivator available to organizations. These are the managers who feel they can field only a mercenary army, an army bought and paid for to do its job. This is probably the most widespread of all managerial attitudes, even today. And when managers project it, workers accept it, and the circle goes round and round.

No one will deny that money is important. Most of us *do* work in a money economy, and cash is the most flexible, most useful medium of exchange we have. People *will* work for money. And for more money. And for more money. And for more. For most people, money has become more than a medium of exchange useful in economic transactions; it has become a badge of honor—and a device for measuring power and for determining the winners of conflicts.

Money does motivate, then, but only for a short time and only as long as it serves as a measure of worth or of power or of victory. But when a given amount of money paid in a particular way begins to lose its symbolic value, the only recourse for the employee is to seek more. The demand for more is not related to amount produced or some personal concept of equity, but to the very human need to be recognized, to be accorded some special distinction. When the only inducement to effort in support of a cause is money, only significant and regular increases in money will keep people at their tasks—and even then often grudgingly.

WILLING COMMITMENT

The organization with spirit, with high morale, with the vivacious-ness that will sustain it despite disappointments and failures is an organization that has in its ranks people who have freely identified themselves with the organization and its goals. On a small scale, then, an organization, whether it's a company, a hospital, a college, or whatever, has the same governing task as a city, a state, or a country: It must conduct its affairs in such a way as to attract to it people who accept its philosophy and purpose and who will will-ingly give their support to achieve the greatest good for all.

Men have long experimented with different political systems in an effort to find one that works. The ingenuity of man has been turned to that task, and from this pool of creativity a variety of "solutions" have arisen. At the moment, political institutions that allow the voices of the citizens of a community to be heard on matters that affect them seem to be the institutions that produce the highest level of general satisfaction—spirit, morale—and the most willing subordination of selfish interest to the interests of the group.

The lessons learned from political science are supported by behavioral science research in industry. The basic structure of most industrial commercial organizations is, of course, hierarchical and authoritative, reflecting the reality of managers being accountable for the prudent use and preservation of the owner's property. But having allowed for reasonable controls to ensure the protection of the property rights of owners, more and more organizations are actively enlisting the participation of their employees in the deci-sion-making processes of the company.

As with political decisions, not everyone participates in all decisions, but as far as possible, those likely to be affected by a decision are asked to express their views and preferences on what decisions should be made. This style of management extends from the highest level of the organization down to the shop floor, and it is known as participative management. In the '30s, in fact, in the context of the emerging union movement in the United States, it was encompassed under the name industrial democracy.

INDUSTRIAL DEMOCRACY

Industrial democracy, today, describes efforts to give employees more control and influence over their own work lives. In some efforts it can involve decisions that range from the design of the work area to who will become members of a work group and how much they will be paid.

This movement toward greater participation of employees in the decisions that affect their everyday work lives—not the politically oriented power thrust of some movements toward "industrial democracy"—seems to reflect the desire of free men to have greater control of their own lives. To the extent that this occurs, and to the extent that free men commit themselves to the goals of the organization because of their participation in its decisions, we are likely to have organizations of spirited, vivacious people working together to accomplish their common goals—not bossed, not "hired," but free, committed men.

In the competitive test of organizations, *jīngshen* counts.   [1978]

5   *Credibility: The Stamp of a Leader*

Every leader needs credibility. It is the coin of communication; without it, his words and actions are worthless.

Followers, too, depend upon a leader's credibility. They want to believe in the cause to which their lives are tied—whether it is in politics, a union, a profession, a charitable organization, a corporation, or some other endeavor. To protect their self-esteem, they need to believe in the leaders of their organization.

Building up a fund of credibility with followers and others requires consistently open and honest behavior over a period of time. Such a reserve will support a manager in time of conflict and often win the day. Say, for example, that there is a dispute in which the manager says. "Yes, it's so," and his adversary says, "No, it isn't." Without this reserve of credibility, the manager may lose both the dispute and the support of his followers.

OPEN TO ATTACK

A manager's credibility is always open to attack—legitimately and otherwise. Those who have watched rival managers "play politics" know that a winning move is to destroy the other's credibility in the eyes of higher management. Doing so effectively will reduce his rival's influence and may even push him down or out of the organization—leaving a clearer path of advancement for the survivor.

Underhanded or unfair attacks of this sort are nurtured in an overheated atmosphere of competitiveness—however good the intent was in fostering competition. Desperate to get ahead, one rival may misrepresent the facts of a situation bearing on the other's credibility. This may be done covertly so that the other has no chance for rebuttal. Another way is through the judicious selection and slanted presentation of statistics; where the others involved are unsophisticated in their use or don't have access to all of them, the strategy often succeeds. Or it can be as simple as calling a meeting and not informing others of agenda items in which facts are involved.

TWO LESSONS

There are at least two lessons here. One is to protect your own credibility. If actions or words signal that it is imperiled, work to find out why and correct the situation. The other lesson is to avoid fostering the kind of "go get 'em" competitiveness that makes one subordinate go for another's jugular.

A manager's credibility with subordinates is particularly important; at stake, of course, is getting the job done. If he demonstrates a lack of credibility, his subordinates will display their disregard of him—a disregard that will show up in absenteeism, late completion of assignments, even subtle sabotage.

THE BASIC STEPS

Although it is sometimes difficult to achieve and maintain credibility, the basic steps are easy to identify:

1. *Tell the truth.* What is true at one time, of course, may not be true later; and what is true to one person may not be true to another. No one can deal in absolute truth—a matter that has engaged philosophers for ages. But you must say what you *believe* at the time to be true. Failing to do so indicates an intention to deceive—whether planned or not. Any inconsistency between what you believe and what you hope another will believe (as a result of what you do or say) destroys credibility. The balance sheet that doesn't present what you know are the facts, the union member who calls in sick when he is not, the mechanic who supplies unneeded services—all these reflect lies. Once discovered, they can irretrievably destroy credibility.

2. *Don't routinely act as though you doubt the other person's credibility.* Until evidence proves otherwise, give him or her the benefit of the doubt. "Management by suspicion" not only counteracts motivational efforts, it also invites mutual suspicion. It prevents you from accruing that important fund of credibility.

3. *Admit mistakes.* Managers are human. When you say, "I was wrong," it strengthens your credibility when you say, "I'm right."

4. *When you don't know something, say so.* If you don't say so, your ignorance will trip you up nine times out of ten. The small advantage that might be gained by bluffing is far outweighed by the possibility of losing your credibility.

5. *Always keep promises.* The reaction to a simple lie may range from annoyance to rage. But it pales beside the reaction to a broken promise, which makes the other person feel cheated.

Credibility is believability. One of the highest—and most beneficial—accolades for a manager is the comment, "If he says so, you can bank on it."   [1976]

6   *Leadership and the Work Ethic*

Leaders should lead—by example. Words may exhort but example quietly persuades and inspires. Ideally, words and example should coalesce. Consistency between words and behavior—that is, a lack of hypocrisy—steels many executives to demand the performance required by the implicit contract that underlies each employee-company relationship. If the work ethic has been in decline in American industry, then, perhaps it is because those who by their own behavior should be showing the way have been shirking their jobs.

There has been much talk in recent years about the many crimes that are committed day by day against business. That crimes against business are a major problem is too well documented to belabor. But I think the most pervasive and damaging of all crimes against business doesn't involve material goods at all. It concerns the theft of productive time by employees who arrive late, read the daily newspaper at their desks, spend much time on personal telephone calls and social visiting, take long lunch hours, or leave the office early—and not only on Friday afternoons.

On hearing such a catalog of "sins," many managers rear back and say with great force, "Yes, it's terrible what has been happening with young people these days. No discipline, no discipline at all." (And it does seem true that some employees object to any restriction on their personal freedom—they prefer the unsupervised society.) Other managers explode with condemnations of the restrictive practices of unionized groups.

These charges undoubtedly contain some truth, and in some situations they may be very true indeed. But in other cases it might be better if these same managers were to look at their own behavior, at the model they present to their employees, before they condemn too loudly. Leaders show the way. If they are true leaders, they are at their desks in the morning as their employees arrive and at their desks in the evening as they leave.

When a poor organizational climate or an employee's prior experience overwhelms the effects of a leader's efforts, costly abuses of understood work standards occur. Such abuses seem to stem from a lack of appreciation of the implicit *quid pro quo* in the employment relationship. The average corporation today employs 10 percent more executives, for example, than it really needs simply because many skimp on their job time. At lower organizational levels the percentage is probably even higher. This ultimately causes top-heavy payrolls and higher consumer prices. No organization can long survive such a loss of competitive edge, and when this loss occurs, not only do the individuals who have shirked go down, but so does the whole team. Organizations don't have watertight doors: An organization's employees either sail together or sink together.

Employees' work attitudes are a function of both where they have been and where they are. A manager hiring a new employee obviously can't control where he or she has been, but such a manager can just as obviously make every effort to learn what each candidate's attitudes have become as a result of these early experiences. A manager should not hire a person who does not evidence a responsible attitude toward work and a willingness to contribute his or her time and talents to the job. Screening employees in terms of their work attitudes—and in keeping with EEO requirements—is an auspicious start toward overcoming employee malaise.

THE IMPORTANCE OF EXAMPLE

However, even employees of good backgrounds and with a strong commitment to work may not perform because of their work climate. The company environment they find when they first report to work can affect their willingness to extend themselves in their new jobs.

The first days on a job are critical in this regard. In selecting a new employee, a manager may have made a special point, for example, of explaining work hours, schedules, and other standards of performance. If when the employee reports to work, however, he or she finds that no one does the things he or she had been told would be expected, which message do you think will be most influential? If a new employee has been told that the workday runs from 9:00 to 5:00 but most people stroll in at 9:30, when do you think the new employee will arrive in a few days? If most employees take lunch from 12:00 to 2:00, how long a lunch break do you think the newly hired employee will take? If everyone leaves the office at 4:45, who will stay until 5:00?

The lesson is clear. No matter what employees may have been told, what they see will determine what they will do. What managers must do, therefore, is ensure that the same rules apply to everyone and that these rules are uniformly enforced. To ignore such a fundamental of good management is to invite the very attitudes managers are striving so hard to overcome.

REASONABLE EXCEPTIONS

Having said that the climate into which a new employee is introduced will affect how he or she behaves, I must add that I do not mean to suggest that no variations from the standard pattern are permissible. Some employees work late into the night on assignments. For them to come in at 10:00 the next morning is understandable. Other employees spend weekends or evenings traveling on business. For them, too, reasonable departures from standard schedules are appropriate.

Many people quarrel with the philosophy I have just expressed. Departures from usual business routines by executive-level personnel typically provoke the most outspoken criticism. Reporters and newscasters challenge managers' perquisites with that special verve we all save for favorite targets. But is it fair?

I am sure there are a few executives who steal from their companies, abuse their positions, and take unreasonable personal time away from the job. But I am just as sure that the number who do this is insignificant. More important for us all are the many managers who are terribly underpaid for what they contribute to their companies and to their communities and for the sacrifices they and their families make so they can devote full time to their jobs. Are the few things that companies do to make life a little easier and a little more pleasant for these executives who give so much of themselves really inappropriate? Are steps that companies take to ensure the continuing good health and élan of their executive group really contrary to the best interest of their employees and stockholders? I think not.

CONSISTENCY AND EVENHANDEDNESS

Returning, however, to the fundamental actions managers can take to maintain or reestablish the work ethic in their companies— managers must ensure consistent and evenhanded enforcement of their companies' policies and rules. Such a stance is the essence of managerial integrity. It is also the personification of a company's ethical posture. It is a *sine qua non* of effective leadership.

Enough. To conclude, I do believe that:

- The work ethic can be maintained or reestablished if managers take proper preventative actions rather than engage in after-the-fact punitive responses.
- Company rewards must relate to and be consistent with the kinds of employee performance that demonstrate commitment and effectiveness.
- Promotions should go to those who have already demonstrated by their example that they will set a good example for those around them. Promotions do not create attitudes toward work that were not previously there but rather fix old patterns of behavior.
- If how people work and what people accomplish is important, then those who work effectively should be made leaders so they can serve as models for others.   [1977]

7 An Urgent Need

"We create a sense of urgency," Dick, a partner in one of the more prestigious consulting firms in the United States, and an old friend, replied. He was answering my question of why his firm, and others like it, was so often able to help client organizations. "We work with outstanding organizations with very able managers. While the staff we assign to a client's problems is very able, person for person the members of our assignment teams are rarely significantly more able than the managers in the client company, although we may have special knowledge and skills. But a major contribution we make to a client is providing a sense of urgency."

"What an interesting reply," I thought, But why do outsiders have to bring such a sense of urgency to a company with problems? What is this sense of urgency? Why do so many managers lack it?

These questions stay with me, perhaps because I so often see the lack of a sense of urgency in the organizations with which I work. But what is this "sense of urgency"?

A SENSE OF URGENCY

In simple terms, it means "never putting off until tomorrow what can be done today." It's managers running, not strolling. It's drive. It's energy. It's a desire to get done today things others would take until next week to do. It's momentum. It is thrust. It is an abhorrence of any wastefulness: Saving pennies counts. It's many things, but in a few words, it's an emotional commitment to get important things done in an acceptable way at the lowest feasible cost in the shortest possible time. A sense of urgency is a combination of attitudes and habits often overlooked by those who have only knowledge and skills—and most successful managers have it.

21

The impatience in urgency creates a drive often criticized by those who deplore the "rat race" and by those who believe that nothing really has to be done today. Truly able managers feel that everything that can be done immediately should be done immediately; the attitude of *mañana* of the "comfortable" manager is not permissible. For the able manager, drive and momentum produce a sense of excitement, an important ingredient of accomplishment.

Little things are important to the manager with a sense of urgency because failure in little things means something is less perfect than is desired; urgency is born in the fear of missing perfection. Those who do not have this sense tend to speak only of the "big picture," the level of their comfortable concern, and believe that detail that can be delegated need not be controlled. The manager with a sense of urgency uses clear controls and insists on fast feedback because only with such an information flow can he be sure the job will be done—right.

Urgency emphasizes timeliness. Tomorrow is not soon enough. The sooner the committed manager can see some activity or accomplishment, the quicker he or she can redirect effort to finish the job or "beat the time frame."

Urgency is demanding. It means long hours, rearranged priorities, sometimes even danger to one's well-being. A manager working with a sense of urgency may confuse his or her associates who don't share that manager's drive. If not recognized and controlled, a strong sense of urgency can lead a manager to be unfair to others who cannot sustain the pace.

Urgency demands innovation and flexibility. It pushes people to try new ideas and shortcuts and to juggle many activities at the same time. It emphasizes prudence in the use of money and time: Resources are to be invested, not spent.

BY NATURE, BUT NURTURED

I think the attitudes and habits that underlie a sense of urgency are laid down early in a manager's life. But I think, too, that the ways organizations are managed stimulate or dampen such drive.

All organizations search continuously for those few outstanding managers who combine knowledge and intelligence with drive and commitment. But with so few about, and so much to be done, an organization must adopt a style that will bring out the best from all its managers. The use of management by objectives, profit centers, participation, delegation, openness to communication up and down, incentives, and so on—all programs designed to get the best in the many to supplement the best from the few—produce a management style that leads to a higher level of urgency in all of an organization's managers—and to a much more effective organization.

Comfortable managers are not great builders. Managers who have accomplished against odds, who have persevered and prevailed, who have urgently striven and advanced, these are the managers who make our future. Their reward? The joy of realizing themselves—for them an urgent need.   [1977]

8   *Wanted: A Sense of Mission*

Hank Viscardi is chairman and president of the Human Resources Center, an organization devoted to helping handicapped individuals enter the mainstream of economic life. Hank has two artificial legs, but he has achieved more with his life than most people without such a disability ever do. And when you visit Hank, you can only be inspired by his enthusiasm for and his commitment to his work. Although already well into his 60s, he's giving no thought to retirement or to slowing his pace. He is a man with a mission. And this seems to be the source of his near boundless energy.

Hank's sense of mission and his obvious enthusiasm for his work are two characteristics that distinguish him from the average run of managers. Another is his creativity. And Hank *gives* his talents to his work. He doesn't do his work for his pay; he takes his pay so he can do his work. Perhaps Hank has something to teach us all.

THE WELLSPRING

A sense of mission is a wellspring of energy. It is a sense of mission that causes people to drive ahead, often against great obstacles, until the job is done. Short-run disappointments and failure prod them to work harder. Their pay sustains them but doesn't spur them. And the excellence of their work is a measure of the importance of their mission.

Many managers are "for hire." They measure their worth, not in terms of the importance of their tasks or their contribution, but rather in terms of their paychecks. These are the managers who want to work at a "good job" rather than to work to build a good life—a contributing life. A "good job" is usually self-centered; it is a job that will enable the person to "better myself," "gain experience," or make "the most logical move" in his or her career plan. And often a "good job" means more money or impressive perks.

Managers who are committed to their jobs believe that what they are doing is, of itself, what they really want to be doing. They seek promotions primarily for the opportunity to do more of what they now do—at a more responsible level. A person who "takes a job" is likely to "do a job," and then look for a change when interest wanes. This is the syndrome that corrupts career planning: Individuals focus on themselves and as a result lose that vital sense of organizational life and purpose.

Events may change the ambitions of any of us. But when we start a job we are asking the rest of the organization and our customers or clients to support us in doing what we want with our lives. To take any job as a stepping-stone to something else is inherently dishonest to supervisors, associates, and subordinates. And it breaks the flow of creative change.

"For hire" managers are always susceptible to the seductions of those who offer money and status to attract them to new jobs. With self-advancement their principal goal, a sense of mission is a distracting irrelevancy. But a price they pay is an incapacity to provide inspired, creative leadership to their organization. Hank is not "for hire." And he is an inspired, creative leader. He's the kind of CEO his organization—any organization—needs.

ORGANIZATIONAL CREATIVITY

Creative leaders encourage creativity. They respect it, nurture it, and use it. Their organizations are structured to encourage creative and flexible approaches to work. Hank has done this, and it is a special strength.

Many managers manage "by the book" or "by the expert." They don't really grow in their jobs or learn from their experiences. They will do tomorrow what they did yesterday because someone told them it was what to do.

Other managers discount completely the advice of "experts," whether presented in books, classes, or face-to-face discussions. These managers so value their freedom—or their own ideas of right or wrong ways to manage—that they prefer to "do it my way." They often think they're being creative, and they often find their work exciting. But those who work with such managers may see them as more stubborn than creative.

Neither a rigid adherence to formulas nor a total disregard of tested precepts can make for effective management. Management is the creative and flexible application of tested principles to particular circumstances.

In his excellent book, *Managing in Turbulent Times*, Peter Drucker states: "Fundamentals do not change. But the specifics to manage them do change greatly with changes in internal and external conditions." He also speaks of the necessity of management being able to adapt to sudden changes and to avail itself of new opportunities. The message is clear: Management must stay flexible. This concept of management as a means to an end rather than an end in itself releases organizational creativity.

While management does not provide as much opportunity for creativity as art or music, it cannot be unimaginative. Those who try to paint a management picture "by the numbers" will always be amateurs. Great artists generally have a deep knowledge of perspective, color, design, and form. They create within these principles—or they may create with the full realization that they are defying the principles. Such controlled creativity is a product of creative leadership.

DEVELOPING CREATIVITY

Creativity can be developed—over time. Alex Osborn, advertising executive and author, demonstrated that. His two books, *Your Creative Power* and *Applied Imagination,* are full of ideas on how people can be helped to become more creative. But developing creativity requires great care and infinite patience.

Internal management practices may hamper even the most innovative employees. For example, well-intentioned staff services—often in a matrix structure—can frustrate innovative efforts. Decentralization can unfetter minds and stimulate innovation. But staff controls can restrict and dampen creative energy. Creative management must blend and balance permissiveness and control if staff/line or matrix structures are to respond creatively to the opportunities decentralization implies.

The sense of freedom generated by decentralization is necessary for a creative organization. There is also a need, however, for organizational controls. Traditional accounting controls that convey the message that only the "bottom line" is real can destroy creativity. But creative controls, controls that accept that management—like control—is not an end in itself, can ensure that the organization stays on course, and afloat.

Hank Viscardi has created this kind of an organization. His sense of mission enables him to give inspired, creative leadership to those with whom he works. His performance would humble many managers in "good jobs." Who's handicapped?   [1980]

9   *NIH: Killer of Creativity*

The entrepreneurial spirit that pervades a new company is an invigorating and infectious thing. Everyone, from the top down, shares an enthusiasm for achievement and a commitment to the goals of the organization. All too often, however, this sense of commitment begins to wither after a while, and creativity withers along with it.

There are several signs by which we can notice this insidious process beginning: Good people resign, offering vague excuses and leaving behind uneasy staffs. Well-qualified job applicants seem interested at first, then politely decline the jobs. There's evidence that people who ought to be working together aren't even communicating—Ed (Production) and George (Marketing) are discovered to be talking to the same clients without each other's knowledge; or Margaret's new packaging concept escapes the attention of the advertising department.

In such cases, the withering agent may be a version of the NIH (Not Invented Here) syndrome that stifles the creativity of many R&D operations. The organization's managers may be saying, in effect, "I don't want any ideas around here that aren't mine!"

If a manager actually pronounced these words, of course, you'd say he was afflicted with a severe case of false pride, limited imagination, or senility. The fact that no one is voicing such feelings openly does not, however, mean that they aren't being communicated somehow to other people in the organization. Here are some phrases that convey the message more subtly but just as surely: "We've tried that once; it didn't work." "Don't let the boss hear that you're monkeying around with that." "You really don't understand the company yet—wait till you've been here a little longer." "Are you trying to make me look bad?"

The NIH virus is bred in company politics and nourished on insecurity. The insecurity may have nothing to do with intelligence; some brilliant people manifest NIH symptoms because they feel chagrined if new ideas come from those they regard as not so brilliant. Often the manager inflicted with the virus is jealously protective of not only his own image but the image of his department as well. "Why didn't *we* think of that?" he is likely to ask his subordinates indignantly.

Under this kind of leadership, creativity dies. People come to care more about protecting what they have than about developing anything new. Surrounded by suspicion and discouraged from open communication, they can't possibly identify with the total organization and its goals.

How can an organization preserve—or regain—the original entrepreneurial spirit and sense of community among its employees? A basic rule for managers is "Pass the pride down." People like to create when they can earn recognition for their ideas. When a good idea surfaces, the creator's immediate superior should show prompt appreciation. Even if he had the same idea himself years before, he should acknowledge that *this* thought at *this* time is the creator's. The message that ought to be communicated down from the highest levels of the organization is that creative achievement makes *everyone* look good.

A necessary accompaniment to pride in achievement is tolerance of mistakes. If people are afraid of criticism, they won't break out of routine. I once saw a sign in a manager's office that read, "We forgive thoughtful mistakes." Underneath that sentence a wag had written, "Once." But isn't it strange how often not even once is permitted?

Finally, a receptive climate for creativity is more likely to exist when managers take the time to think, to listen, and to read about new concepts. If we are familiar with the base from which a new idea is originating, we can more readily accept that new idea. And once we've accepted it, perhaps we won't be so apt to mandate the same old decisions.

An executive once commented to me that too many ideas seem to flow from the top of an organization down and too few from the bottom up. If we are truly supportive, undefensive, and open with our colleagues and subordinates, we will find many more ideas flowing up. These ideas will spark others, and the organization's entrepreneurial spirit will thrive.   [1973]

10 *A Leading Combination*

When we describe a company as having "good management," it goes without saying that it has good leadership as well. If these qualities are not precisely synonymous, they are certainly complementary and so interlocked that the situations in which a manager has no one to lead are rare. An executive assigned to manage a department, a division, or the entire organization is just naturally expected to be a "leader" as well.

Leaders sometimes fail in their roles as managers—you don't have to be a student of history to be able to tick off a few of the more obvious examples. But in business, we should be more curious about why some managers fail as leaders. Our recent elections—like all elections—brought into office some people who will not be good managers. But this deficiency is far more tolerable than instances in which those in managerial roles fail as leaders.

Differentiating between the characteristics of leader and manager is difficult, particularly when you try to assess the qualities in any one person. In general, however, both roles confer on the individual certain degrees of power and recognition, which vary according to the influence of many factors—type of organization, unit structure, level within the structure, and even the timing of one's incumbency. But over all, when mixed with the proper allotment of wisdom, the combination of recognition and power can create a powerful positive force in the organization.

MANAGING LEADERSHIP

In recent years I have had the opportunity to meet many men and women who were in the process of changing managerial jobs. Most knew a great deal about management and liked their positions of

29

managerial power. But what they did not seem to like—or were not ready to accept—were the aspects of leadership with which managers must learn to live.

"Until I got to the top," one man confided to me, "I never encountered jealousy. But I soon learned that some of my colleagues, including many I worked with for years, deeply resent my making it to the top." This manager was so uncomfortable in that environment that he had decided to leave his job.

I heard essentially the same story from others—including two university administrators, a woman leading a religious group, and several business managers. Jealousy and backbiting had caused them to lose faith in the people they were depending on for help in their organizations.

Most leaders easily ride out such conflicts. They may express sorrow that others feel as they do—jealousy, envy, or whatever— but they accept such resentments as part of the burden of leadership. In other words, they learn to live with it.

Managing Critics

Good managers have similar strengths. Those who know that jealousy is "more self-love than hate" can often incorporate jealous rivals into their plans, confident that regardless of personal feelings, these persons will eventually identify with an organizational objective and work for the good of the group. The wise manager tries to build relationships that will permit co-workers to work well with their peers despite any antagonistic feelings toward him.

Both leaders and managers know they are going to be hit with criticism. In the wide social context, David Ben-Gurion termed it "the test of a democracy," and James Russell Lowell saw it as "wise skepticism." But many managers are inclined to share Mark Twain's sentiment that criticism is the "most degraded of all trades."

It should be remembered, however, that organizational decisions are usually made on a series of assumptions and a paucity of facts. Add the elements of time restraint and risk, and it becomes obvious that some judgments will be less than perfect—if not plain wrong— thus inviting critical reaction.

Of course, such reaction ranges from friendly and helpful—though critical—advice to outright abuse, and at midrange it is often difficult to determine whether criticism is helpful or abusive. Many executives confuse productive criticism with negativism or fail to give their decision-making processes sufficient time to digest wise criticism. Thus they soon tire of what they see as "sniping" by employees, consumers, government officials, and even fellow managers. In short, they fail to respond effectively to pressure.

Leaders generally choose a life filled with pressures voluntarily. Harry Truman's famous dictum—"If you can't stand the heat . . ."—fits well here. The managerial side of leadership responds to the heat by deft organization, honest negotiations, and well-determined priorities—thus absorbing the pressure for action on matters that cannot be dealt with immediately.

WHEN FORESIGHT FAILS

Most pressures, however, do not develop suddenly and can be averted by foresight and planning. Occasionally a confluence of totally unpredictable events will yield a crisis. Though a leader may not be at fault in such emergencies, he or she is responsible for them: It's the burden of leadership. In such situations, the leader must be able to react with "grace under pressure"—which was Ernest Hemingway's definition of courage. In a crisis, the true leader or successful manager does not engage in petty name-calling or finger-pointing; he or she absorbs the pressure with good grace and uses the experience as a guidepost for the future.

PLACING THE BLAME

Humorist Fran Lebowitz has observed: "It's not whether you win or lose but how you lay the blame." This consolation, however, is denied the true leader. The demands of leadership are heavy: The true leader must be able to rise above the emotional vindictiveness of others; to accept accountability for the unforeseeable; to pitch headlong into the swirling, threatening currents of change.

The changing nature of a job provides some managers with a

reason for resigning. In most cases, the job should have changed years ago, but any movement was delayed until, say, a merger or new president spotlighted the necessity for a change in direction or emphasis. Most of us sometimes experience lazy streaks and want the world to stand still, but a leader can't afford this luxury. On the contrary, leaders maintain momentum by introducing change—which so often is the only way to get from here to there.

Some managers who decide they must switch jobs are those who have reached the limit of their management capacity and are unable to continue at levels beyond their competence. Others want out for reasons peculiar to their individual situations. In the end, however, I am still fascinated by how often reaction to jealousy, sensitivity to criticism and pressure, and resistance to change are cited as the primary reasons for quitting. However legitimate these reasons may be, their overall sum is rationalization. The manager who quits is not just confessing distaste for aspects of the job but is demonstrating inability to measure up to the basic qualities of managerial leadership.   [1978]

11   *An Exemplary Performance in Management*

How much is a manager worth as measured by the values of his or her organization? Is this value different from the price society would establish for similar leadership?

The answer to the first question can be obtained relatively easily because there are many ways to estimate what a manager should be paid by his or her business—sales volume, profitability, size of budget, number of people supervised, position in the organization, and so on. If any or all of these criteria were the basis for paying for a manager's decision-making chores between nine and five each day, determining a fair level of compensation would be easy . . . and it would be a relatively modest sum. Few would receive what could be regarded as a fabulous amount.

MANAGERS ARE LEADERS

But managers have a broader role as leaders. And for that reason, their influence can—and often does—extend far beyond their organizational boundaries. A few may be seen by society as worthy of imitation, as models for human relationships not only on the job but in other facets of person-to-person experiences. Many more managers are imitated at the office or plant level by middle managers and first-line supervisors, who—in their own daily contacts both on and off the job—also affect society in countless ways.

It's difficult to dwell on the personalities of the executives who sit as the chairman or president of IBM, Du Pont, Bank of America, or British Airways without acknowledging that by virtue of their position they have accepted an obligation to set an example for others not only within their own corporations but outside the companies as well. For executives in smaller companies, this beyond-the-job obligation may be to their local communities. Under normal circumstances, a community is generally proud of its leaders, and managers are almost invariably among them.

In the public sector a manager's overall responsibilities have a similar, though perhaps more direct, impact because these broader responsibilities automatically accompany public life. The mayor of Sacramento, the superintendent of schools in Boston, the librarian in Peoria are watched for what they do and don't do, for what they say and don't say, at least within their own municipal, regional, or functional areas.

SETTING AN EXAMPLE

In a word, then, any manager's obligation goes far beyond directing a team to get results, because as a leader, a manager automatically shoulders the need to set an example. And good example plays a key role in building effective business teams.

The need to set an example is a requirement that outstanding

leaders have always emphasized. The British statesman Lord
Clarendon pointedly observed: "No man is so insignificant as to be
sure his example can do no harm." Benjamin Franklin called
example the "best sermon." The heroic Albert Schweitzer put the
challenge to managers clearly on the line when he said that "example is not the main thing in life—it is the only thing."

Thus for some, managers are heroes to be imitated. For others,
they are bosses to be obeyed. This admiration, ideal or pragmatic,
exists as part of what we now call organizational culture. The
manager who is rejected as an example to be followed tends to drive
members of the team to imitate other leaders.

Leadership and its requirement to set an example impose obligations and disciplines that may be difficult to accept. And society—
standing apart from the plant and office—may see this criterion
better than managers or their employees. Too many managers
accept a promotion as simply the route to more money, more status,
more people to whom they can say "Do as I say."

A religious leader I know asserted that he would never ask one of
his aides to do anything he would not be willing to do himself.
"Doesn't that deprive you of the time you need for managing?" I
asked. Reiterating that he would "do anything" any of his people do
"if I must," he answered: "They know that I have had jobs like theirs
and did them—or at least endured them. I go down where they are,
where their frustrations are. They don't want me to do their
jobs, but they want to be sure I know what it's like when they do
them."

My friend explained further that there are "dirty parts to all jobs."
He hoped to get out of the fishbowl in which he lived. He wanted a
little privacy, no telephones, a beer in peace, and a seat at a
ballgame at which no one recognized him. The essence of what he
said is that example is not what we do once or only today; it is a
record that many can see—a habit, a trait. Example has a lasting
quality that a team will not forget.

MANAGERIAL SACRIFICES

It is sad that we can find so many managers who forget all about
good example and manage their executive bailiwicks with the

spoken—or implied—admonition, "Don't do as I do; do as I say." Managers who abdicate leadership in this way would have us believe that if they can make correct decisions regularly, then they are free as individuals to do as they please. They make the rules, but are not necessarily bound by them. They regard their behavior, erratic or not, as a privilege of office as long as they get results. Are we, or are we not, they say, entitled to our private lives?

Those who accept promotion to manager or to some higher level in management must realize that the step up more often than not will abridge private life, involve family as never before, and sometimes expose the recipient of promotion to criticism and abuse. It changes the number of hours in the day, reorients social relationships, and extends the limits of boredom. It can destroy anonymity. It's not easy for many would-be young managers to accept such requirements.

Whether it's a president chosen by a board of directors or a first-line supervisor selected after an assessment process, delegation of authority to anyone is effective only when that authority is accepted in the spirit in which it was given. Some managers might assume that they were being asked to do a good job only on the company's business, narrowly defined. But is that what was intended in all cases?

Might not the idea have been to select a new leader to represent the company in the community, to carry a new image of the company abroad?

SHARING THE CREDIT

Example does not always rise to dramatic proportions. If we would give creative opportunity to imaginative people at the bottom of the organization, we must encourage such efforts by our organizational and personal receptivity to new ideas. If we want civility, we must act civilized. If we want to judge fairly, we must show both justice and mercy.

Perhaps the best example of the successful manager is the quiet one. Quiet personalities produce other quiet managers, who let people get credit for what they do no matter where it all began. These are the ones of whom Lao-tzu wrote:

A leader is best
When people barely know he exists,
Not so good when people obey and acclaim him,
Worse when they despise him.
Fail to honor people,
They fail to honor you,
But of a good leader, who talks little,
When his work is done, his aim fulfilled,
They will all say, "We did this ourselves."

[1981]

PART TWO

Character

12   Fortitude, Patience, Courage

"Thank God for the iron in the blood of our fathers," said Theodore Roosevelt, a not unexpected epigram from a leader who thrived on the joys of striving against adversity for high goals. And if he gave thanks for the fortitude of his forebears, so should we—particularly in July. We, too, have received many gifts from those who have gone before us, gifts of independence and freedom acquired by dedicated people at great cost. And as Roosevelt suggested, perhaps the greatest of these gifts is the gift of fortitude.

Fortitude enables average people to accomplish goals that more able but weaker ones forgo. It underlies perseverance. It walks side by side with patience. And it breaks bread with courage.

VALUES FROM THE PAST

Those who shaped our country more than 200 years ago had fortitude, perseverance, patience, and courage, and the men and women who will shape our country—and its institutions—today must be of the same character. And these leaders are in place, even though they may cast different shadows than leaders in the past because they have been shaped by different events.

A sense of history is important in the makeup of a leader, for those who know the problems mankind has faced in the past and how they were overcome are not dismayed by the problems of today. History teaches us that, although the context may change, people make the difference—and in making the difference, make history. Those who have no knowledge of what mankind has overcome have not yet learned the ability of mankind to prevail.

Look at our own early history. Who would have thought that an ill-equipped, amateur army of poorly educated castoffs from the

39

most powerful nation in the world could withstand the force of arms
of that nation—and prevail? Who has been to the major battle-
grounds of that struggle, and to the winter campground at Valley
Forge, without marveling at the courage of those who fought or
wintered there and persevered to win victory? If people did that in
the past, can't they do it now? They can.

PEOPLE MAKE THE DIFFERENCE

That is the lesson of history. People make the difference. And men
and women today will teach that lesson of history to the men and
women of tomorrow.

Since the world has become so much more complex, it is easy for
us to throw up our hands and say that no one person makes a
difference. It is also easy for those who might do grand deeds to
sorrowfully note that the opportunities to be great are fewer today
than they were in the past. That is true; there is more good
competition today. It is also true that, if we are looking for fame, it is
harder to attain—unless you can hit four home runs in a World
Series. But most worthwhile struggles are won by the organized
efforts of countless unknown people who act with fortitude, patience, and courage.

These are the people who have retained their dreams of what
their community might and should be. They have not turned their
backs on the larger problems of the world, but they have turned
their faces to the problems close at hand about which they *can* do
something—and they are doing it. These people are making history.

Think, too, of the unknown workers who have preserved their
integrity and carry their ethics with them to the office or factory
each day—despite the headlines that suggest corruption is endemic.
The issues they face may not make news; they only involve matters
of honesty and truthfulness and courtesy. But by staying true to
their beliefs and working courageously to make these beliefs prevail, these people are making history.

Think, too, of the legislators who face daily the choice of voting
their conscience or of bowing to the pressures of expediency. Those

who vote their conscience make history—even when they are wrong on the particular issue. Being "right" on an issue is not critical; being right about the importance of the individual's conscience as the determinant of actions taken is. Preserving conscience gives strength.

And think of the parents who love their children enough to say no. And to say no again. And again. And to continue saying no until the request fits their values and concern for what is right, not for what happens to be popular at the moment. Their children may rebel. They will certainly turn the full force of their neighborhood's mores on their parents, and they will certainly threaten to withhold their love. But with fortitude, the parents persevere. Here again, being right isn't the issue; the integrity of the parents' beliefs and their willingness to stand against those who disagree, not self-righteously, but humbly yet firmly, these are what will make history.

With such people as these, there is no cause for despair about our future.

VALUES FOR THE FUTURE

Nor is it always a matter of looking back for our values. During the 1950s and 1960s, and even to this day, men and women have had to persevere to make their vision of the future prevail. Who would have predicted 50 years ago that as a nation we would overcome so much of our infamous history of racial and religious discrimination? But we have accomplished much to erase the blight on our nation because a handful of brave people—leaders who too often are lost to history—had a vision of the future, knew what was right, had the fortitude to persevere. But the struggle isn't over. The methods used may be imperfect, but the goal is shared.

The issue here is fundamental. Personal values and character were important in leaders 3,000 years ago, 1,000 years ago, and 200 years ago. They remain important today and will always be important. There is nothing old-fashioned about values. They are not like clothing fashions, here today and changed tomorrow. They are stable and lasting because they are addressed to the nature of man. Whether alone or in groups, people share a common psychology and similar human needs.

Fortitude is important because we all need constancy before a challenge as an anchor for our own wavering hearts—a fearfulness that is the common lot of mankind.

Patience, too, is important and a mark of character to which we all respond because we know that worthwhile things are rarely accomplished quickly. In any large group there are many different interests to be satisfied. To accomplish this takes prolonged negotiation, and negotiating takes time.

HOEING THE FIELDS

Perseverance is the telltale mark of dedication, and without dedication there is nothing. What truly worthwhile things are easy to achieve? None. Worth, in fact, is measured by difficulty, and the inevitable correlate of difficulty is the need for perseverence. It is easy to start difficult tasks; it is hard to continue when the frustration of failure and the disappointment of high expectations not fulfilled mount hour by hour, day by day, and year by year. The test of the farmer is not in planting the seed but in hoeing the weeds from the fields. Most of us like to plant; few of us like to hoe. But it is in the hoeing—in persevering—that the crop is made.

And courage. What can be said about courage that has not already been said? It is not the courage of the battle, or the courage of the crisis, that is of concern—although those kinds of courage are also important. No, the courage that counts is the courage to do your job day by day, quietly, without recognition, often without hope, sustained only by the realization that you are doing something that matters to you and to others. And it is the courage to listen and learn from criticism—and to persevere. That is the kind of courage we need in boundless supply in our country today.   [1978]

13   *Character*

Character is what we are; reputation is what others think we are. Fulton J. Sheen said it graphically: "Man is very much like a barrel of apples. The apples that are seen on the top are his reputation, but the apples down below represent his character." So too for managers and their organizations.

To friends and competitors, our reputation is our presence when we are absent or not involved. And many who know nothing of our organization or our people may know us only through our reputation. A reputation is a message about us that grows and travels by word of mouth. Big corporations, of course, expect their reputations to bring them recognition around the world. On a somewhat smaller scale, this is equally true of individual managers: To be known as a "good manager" or "a real pro" is a great asset.

Organizations in the United States invest prodigiously to build favorable reputations. And this spending is not confined only to profit-making organizations. Colleges and universities publish materials that tell of their academic or sports accomplishments. They even arrange commencements to force the world to pay attention. Governments, too, spend millions of tax dollars to tell taxpayers what they are doing—a fascinating aspect of all bureaucracies. Airports, new municipal construction, and public buildings, all display conspicuously the names of the architect, of the members of the legislative commitee that authorized the construction, and of the mayor or governor. While they may all be people of character, reputation is obviously also a major—perhaps a predominant—concern.

A REPUTATION IS FRAGILE

"A reputation once broken may possibly be repaired, but the world will always keep its eye on the spot where the crack was." This quotation from *Supervision* emphasizes the fragility of a reputation. And this fragility is why managers should be uncompromising on character, the only sound foundation for a reputation. Under the worst of circumstances, when an organization's or a manager's reputation is under attack, character provides a basis for serenity. Today a reputation can be fractured so easily by a harsh investigative reporter, a zealous politician, a crusading consumer, or a greedy stockholder. An upright character is the best defense in these situations.

The character of any organization is the character of its managers and employees. The first ingredients of character are integrity and honesty. Most people who look for honesty and integrity in organizations assume humans are not perfect in everything they do; they are not sanctimonious in their attitudes. But they also assume that people are honest, even about their mistakes and lapses.

PUBLIC IMAGE, PRIVATE SUBSTANCE

I watched a president explain to his board of directors the discovery of the criminal acts of one of his most trusted subordinates. His pain was caused, not only by the embarrassment of the incident, but also by the necessary dismissal of a friend. The entire organization was watching and speculating. Do we have the character to withstand the negative consequences if this incident gets into the newspapers and besmirches our reputation? I also watched a president strongly defend a vice-president when someone on his board felt that a gossip column exposé threatened the reputation of the company. The president believed the rumors were unfounded. He was right; the vice-president was later vindicated.

Both these presidents showed character. Difficult decisions are much easier to make when made in the context of a firm character.

How would you or I answer if asked, "What is this organization *really* like when no one is looking?" "Is the organization doing the 'right' thing because it is right—or to create a good impression?" If I could say that we act the same in inconspicuous isolation as in the glare of publicity, and we act "right" because it is right, I would feel great pride in my organization.

Do we believe that an objective examination of our companies would reflect concern for people, their futures, their compensation, their fair treatment? Would we be giving equal treatment to all comers if it were not required by law? Do we reward good performers and give poor ones every chance before we allow them to be separated? Are fringe benefits viewed as earned and just compensation to employees in today's society or are they something "they" must bargain for? Do we tell our board members the bad news as well as the good? Would we oppose a popular proposition that in our judgment violated an important ethical principle?

We could go on and on raising such questions. We need to ask, for example, questions about the bottom line and wasteful management practices. Managers of character are constantly asking questions like these. They believe they should be answered by managers within the firm long before anyone outside the firm asks them. And answers that challenge the integrity of the organization must be faced forthrightly and necessary changes made.

Organizational—or personal—postures that emphasize character are not easy today. Some adversaries are only too willing to fracture a reputation to gain a selfish end. But good union members, dedicated consumers, serious stockholders, concerned employees, and a fair press can help make character count by respecting and supporting individuals and companies that display it. They understand and respect such simple statements as "We made a mistake" or "Yes, your information is correct—we goofed." In a well-run, highly decentralized company, thousands of events are taking place every day. For any manager to assume he or she can know about all these events and approve or disapprove them is fantasy. Often the public does not understand this.

Some of the questions being asked by the public and particularly by young people are an attempt to find character in organizations. They read and hear about reputation. But they do not understand why the billboards announce the marvels of a product for which it is almost impossible to obtain service. A "rip-off," in fact, can be viewed as the inconsistency between reputation and what you really get for your money. So, while public relations officers may extol the character of their organizations, the people pay little heed since, for them, character is apparent only in terms of their own experiences—which too often belie the press releases.

SEARCHING FOR CHARACTER

Some large companies do work hard at making decisions that reflect character. My personal experiences with IBM, Nabisco, and the Bell System—to pick three at random—have persuaded me that these organizations have great character and are fully deserving of admiration. But we all know other large organizations that are almost bankrupt in character. Such organizations hurt the image of business and give rise to questions about the enterprise system.

Adherence to tested ethical principles is supportive of organizational character. In 1954, when AMA made ethical considerations a major element in its management course, I was impressed enough to look for outlines for a course in business ethics for use in a college curriculum. Professor Herbert L. Johnston at Notre Dame had the best outline for such a course—one of the very few I could find. Today all universities suddenly believe ethics should be in the young manager's curriculum. As a result, the future will be better. However, most managers and university business course teachers *have* awakened a bit late. Perhaps they are still seeking reputation, not character. But the survival of business depends on more than reputation.   [1978]

14   *The Gentle Use of Power*

Recently I visited Washington and Lee University at Lexington, Virginia. A landmark institution that boasts close ties to both its namesakes—George Washington was one of its early benefactors, and Robert E. Lee served as its president from 1865 to 1870—it is rich in the history and traditions of our country and the region where it is situated.

One of the stories told visitors to the W&L campus relates how the courtly former Confederate commander responded to a new student who asked for information about the university's rules—the do's and don'ts governing the conduct of its all-male student body. Lee's reply exemplified the dignity that distinguished the career of this famous leader. There is only one rule, Lee is reported to have said—"that you act as a gentleman."

LESSON FOR TODAY

Some years later, historians found Lee's definition of a gentleman written in his own hand. The Virginian's words carry a message for every manager—male or female—in today's business world.

> The forbearing use of power does not only form a touchstone . . . the manner in which an individual enjoys certain advantages over others is a test of a true gentleman.
>
> The power the strong have over the weak, the employer over the employed, the educated over the unlettered, the experienced over the confiding, even the clever over the silly—the forbearing or inoffensive use of all this power or authority, or a total abstinence from it when the case admits it, will show the gentleman in a plain light. The gentleman does not needlessly and unnecessarily remind an offender of a wrong he may have committed against him. He can not only forgive, he can forget; and he strives for that nobleness of self and mildness of character which impart sufficient strength to let the past be but the past. A true man of honor feels humbled himself when he cannot help humbling others.

If we substitute the word "manager" for "gentleman"—and assume that today's manager includes "lady"—this rather long description says much about managerial power. It imparts, of course, the best tone of *noblesse oblige*, which—translated into late twentieth century terminology—also applies to managers. They also should be aware that they have a similar obligation to the society in which they are leaders—not to stress any special privilege.

THE NEED FOR "ATTITUDE"

We are often reminded, however, that in these hectic (less dignified?) times we are doing less than we should to make certain that our upcoming managers recognize and acquire the distinguishing hallmark of character that Lee required of his undergraduates in the similarly turbulent late 1860s. It is unfortunate that so much of what is written today about management fails to deal with the basic issue of personal attitude toward power and the attendant social responsibilities that are laid upon those who attain it.

We try to legislate in the area of social responsibility and, accordingly, we try to teach the basis for its requirements under law. But I am not sure that our formal education of managers has really done a good job here. There is a deficiency in our educational system—at no level is the development of attitudes really regarded as important, and we tend to tiptoe in the shallows of social responsibility.

Even at advanced levels, in our courses in ethics, we tend to measure progress, not by changes in the attitudes of the student himself, but rather in the knowledge acquired or in the judgments displayed for evaluating others.

In addition, our record within organizations is hardly beyond criticism. How can we be surprised that some managers regard success as just "getting results" or as the "marshaling of assets"—and that acquiring power is the best path to a career as a leader? Among such managers, to regard power as a "gentleman" might be construed as a weakness.

And how strange that this abuse of power so often appears in the middle- or lower-management ranks. What a waste to teach human relations as knowledge, or even as sensitivity to others, only to find that, in practice, the manager wields his power with a rough hand, failing to sense any of the obligations of a "gentleman." It makes a course in human relations little better than a course in plumbing.

MANAGERIAL "TAIL-TWISTERS"

Yet, tradition does continue as a vital force. Most of the great managers I have known would meet Lee's definition of a "gentleman." Most are highly sensitive to others; almost unaware of their influence, they are surprised when they realize that others perceive them as powerful. Mostly, however, they feel "humbled when they cannot help humbling others."

But we do meet managers who believe that having power requires them to be "hard-nosed" and permits them to overlook their
rudeness, crudeness, and indifference to the feelings of others,
particularly their subordinates and others in the workforce.

A young woman, who had just entered the training field, once
wrote me a letter in which she was extremely critical; she injected a
"let's twist the tiger's tail" tone into her complaint. So sure was she
of her professional status that she sent carbon copies to her vice-
president and president.

Letters of complaint are a regular, if regretted, part of every
manager's life. Some are structured to be our most valuable tools in
taking corrective action, and we can appreciate critics who have a
good basis for their remarks. But destructive letters bring a touch of
sadness to the manager who knows what power means.

In the case of the young woman who wrote the letter, all the
evidence indicated she was wrong, and her criticism was answered
in a full explanation. And just about then, another letter arrived—
from my critic's president, who expressed regret about the incident.
He described his employee as a "brilliant young lady," but said he
believed she never should have written what she did. In effect, she
had used the power of a customer in an irresponsible way; without
realizing it, she had embarrassed a gentleman, her boss.

Behaviorists tell us much about poor management practices—
reprimanding in the presence of others; not listening because we
can't wait to talk; ridiculing, demeaning, and ignoring good people
whose position may be different from ours. These personnel practices are bad, not just because of what they do to others; they are
also bad because of what they tell us about the manager who would
engage in them.

THE GOOD OLD DAYS

Some say that the courtesy and politeness that marked social and
business relationships in the past, when social codes were far more
rigid, have disappeared forever—that the days of "ladies and gentlemen" have vanished. Perhaps. But I am fortunate to know many
ladies and gentlemen in all walks of life and in leading organizations.
Many of them are young people who, though they probably never

read the definition penned by Robert E. Lee, are demonstrating
the responsible use of power as he described it.

It is heartening to know that so many of these young managers
generally are among those who make it to the top.   [1978]

15   *The Silent Virtue*

Most of us have heard of the manager whose greatest pride was his
sense of humility. Such ambivalence is characteristic of really great
managers, most of whom eschew the hubris that leads lesser
executives to unhappy ends.

But to the world, the manager so often comes through as sure,
firm, and even arrogant, and the deep sense of humility that
underlies the easy certainty of most great leaders goes unseen. Thus
the decisions that flow from a healthy interplay of authority and
power, involvement and isolation, tend to create a tempting vulner-
ability. Such managers, who prefer to take their work seriously and
not themselves thus assume a posture that makes them a target of
nearly everyone around them—of journalists, scholars, and even
fellow managers. Finding faults in the decisions of other people
must be one of the great managerial indoor sports.

HUMILITY IN THE ORGANIZATION

In organizations, humility is vital to a continuing harmonious operation. It is basic to understanding how much we depend on others
and they on us. It is a vital ingredient of the axiom that "management is the development of people, not the direction of things"—a
principle underscored by Joe D. Batten in his best-selling book,
Tough-Minded Management. "The actions of a responsible executive
are contagious," says Batten. And in the practice of management—
where facts are rare and time is real—most good decisions are a

happy blend of opinions and a few facts constrained by time and then fitted, if necessary and possible, to the people involved. Such variables constantly remind managers of how vulnerable they are.

Teambuilding thus requires a good bit of humility. A good team is a group of people who work well together; it is not a mutual admiration society. No one hears what he or she would most like to hear all the time; a team won't work if any one of its members doesn't believe that others on it know something he or she doesn't. Listening takes great self-discipline and a measure of self-effacement. Selective listening smacks of selective pride.

Too Proud to Learn

Most of us have suffered through the session with the arrogant manager who lets others speak but doesn't really want anything said that he doesn't already know. Mindless closing of communication lines can easily occur when you mix rank with knowledge. First-line supervisors can thus squelch bottom-rung hourly workers, who so often are expected to know little or nothing beyond their own limited job assignment: "This is the way we do it—no ifs, ands, or buts." It also happens at the top where presidents can squelch vice-presidents. People with degrees do it to those with lesser academic credentials, and those with experience sometimes do it when they wish only to repeat experience.

Humility is basic to the learning process. Once we are sure we know it all—most often expressed as disregard or disdain for the thinking and skills of others—our minds are closed.

Brilliant bosses sometimes suffer from this hang-up. But really good managers find excitement in what others can teach—the problems of the less privileged, the ambition of the young, how emotions change thinking, and a thousand other subjects. What a shame that more of our leading managers are too proud to go back for more formal training. New learning has a way of modifying what we thought was certainty. The poor manager places decisions in neat categories and then finds management monotonous because events and people keep fitting into these categories.

Executives who believe that personal development is only for others invariably are arrogant persons. Many of them get this way by the old route of reading their own press releases. Public relations is a great way to build the image of an organization, but operations can be derailed when someone decides to cater to the image of the CEO rather than concentrating on the organization. There will always be CEOs and other top executives who tolerate this—they tend not only to read their press releases but to compound the felony by believing them. When this happens, their own development stops and, worse yet, their development of others also begins to suffer. Although it is not the grandest manifestation of humility, reluctance to be in the news does have virtue. The greatest executives I know shun the spotlight as best they can; they step into the spotlight only when the organization gains, never on a personal basis.

CAUGHT IN THE WEB

But not only the high and mighty can be knocked off pedestals. Lesser folk who become more uppity than common sense would permit are also subject to retribution when they fall victim to a devil's "pride that apes humility."

One mindful executive I know often turns to antiquity to underscore the dangers of losing perspective about one's knowledge, power, and skills as compared with similar attributes in others. One of his favorite tales describes the fate of Arachne, a mythological peasant girl who dared to boast that her ability to weave fine cloth equaled or surpassed that of Athena, who was—among other things—the goddess of that art. The goddess, with typical Olympian arrogance, challenged the mortal to a contest. Both women set up their looms and worked furiously, using skein after skein of gold and silver thread. Both finished their weaving at the same time, and the haughty Athena, confident that her cloth outdazzled that of her mortal rival, turned to look at Arachne's loom. One glance convinced her that she had lost the contest, and, in a fit of fury, the goddess ripped Arachne's work to shreds. Terrified, the girl fled and hanged herself. Later, experiencing remorse, Athena changed the body of Arachne into a spider, belatedly ensuring that the girl's skill in weaving would continue through the ages.

Both goddess and mortal lost in this contest. Athena learned that, despite her Olympian powers, she could not always outperform a mortal; Arachne won the contest but lost her life and was condemned to an eternity of spinning fragile webs. Lack of humility on the part of both goddess and mortal prevented them from learning from each other.

Humility helps us to live sensibly in our society. But if we can't empathize with the lot of others who live in that society with us and if we can't remember some of our own beginnings, government eventually will do what our pride precludes.

Criticism is a good test of humility. (Athena, of course, failed the test, a not unusual outcome in Olympian society.) And with mortal executives the criteria are even more strict. When others are wrong, good executives are disciplined to remain quiet and even be kindly and tolerant. Top managers are good at this. But absorbing what others throw at us—sometimes unfairly—takes courage and self-effacement.

THE LIGHTER SIDE

There's a lighter side to humility. It is what Fulton Sheen describes as "being able to laugh at our own foibles." I recall a manager who insisted on seeing all bills and initialing them before payment. But his initials were illegible, and to mock him, fellow managers started making signs and scratches in place of their signatures on documents.

One day the boss complained that he couldn't figure out who signed anything, and one of his braver colleagues responded: "Neither can we." Everyone laughed. But the manager got the message and soon began to talk delegation and accountability.   [1978]

16 The Power of Patience

Exceptional performance requires vision, imagination, and effort—served by patience, their abiding handmaiden.

An admirer once remarked to the great pianist Paderewski on how much patient effort he must have invested to perfect his art. Paderewski's casual reply is a classic: "Everyone has patience. I learned to use mine."

If they are to perfect their art, managers, too, must have patience. It is frustrating to wait for a plan to come to fruition, a promising subordinate to develop, a team to take shape, a crisis to be resolved. But such matters *will* yield to patience—and sustained effort.

Patience *is* a virtue, but its power is strengthened when it does not stand alone. Augustine, for example, referred to patience as "the companion of wisdom." And Pliny called it "a great part of justice." It is this coupling of patience with other virtues that distinguishes it from apathy.

When the world moved slowly, the pace of events imposed patience. But during the past 100 years, the rate of change has accelerated rapidly, and with it the pace of events and our expectations of the speed of decisions and actions. When messages bounce off satellites at the speed of light, we expect instantaneous responses to questions or efforts. But such decisiveness and quick action do not come because they depend on people—and we haven't changed, really. This conflict between our unrealistic expectations and reality challenges our patience daily.

TESTS OF PATIENCE

For managers, planning provides a test of patience. To spend seemingly endless hours in often repetitious meetings, to cope with mountains of paperwork and page after page of statistical data, to wrestle with contention and uncertainty—these are tests of patience. What document, no matter how accurate and useful, could reflect the care and concern—and patience—of those who created it? A plan is to planning as meeting minutes are to the meeting itself, a poorly focused and partial image of a dynamic process.

The test continues, though. The recorded plan can and often does provoke impatience. Plans—and planning—raise expectations. Members of a planning team have imagined their Rome, and they are in a tearing hurry to see it fully constructed. They want to be at the top of the hill without making the long climb. They're impatient.

The dreams and visions that arise from a planning process are like the pictures on jigsaw puzzle boxes: They show our destination. But the pieces inside the box represent the reality of making our dreams come true. Implementing a plan requires that we take each of the hundreds of pieces of our puzzle and determine where it fits. Slowly, ever so slowly, through patient and sustained effort, the pieces are put into place and the picture takes shape; our vision is realized.

Often the most critical pieces of an organizational planning puzzle involve people. The "right" people are often not in the "right" place. While planning-team members are eager to rush ahead, the manager in charge realizes that delicate job reassignments must be made so the organization's human resources can be deployed more effectively. Such organizational shifts must be handled with care to protect the reputations and feelings of those affected. Long discussions may be necessary; these will inevitably take time and cause delays. And not everyone will know about or understand these delays. This will be a test of patience for all involved.

Grooming managers to move ahead takes time—patience. Most managers grow somewhat like trees, little by little each day, almost undetectably. But after years of such growth, we often find ourselves recalling with wonder the "sapling" that gave us doubts. Like growing trees, growing people is a slow process. Rushing trees and people is a ready formula for weakness and failure.

PEOPLE PATIENCE

The everyday management of people is another test of patience. Sustaining faith in people and in their basic goodness requires thought, effort—and patience. All of us who work in groups are public persons, convenient targets for malicious or recreational gossip. And "keeping track of the boss" is a popular game, among directors as well as workers. The criticisms and rumors that often spring from this game can be terribly unjust.

Such unjust judgments may hurt us, but with understanding and patience we can avoid doing ourselves the greater damage of losing our faith in the basic goodness of those with whom we work. Wise managers remember Seneca's admonition: "He who injured you is either stronger or weaker. If he is weaker, spare him; if he is stronger, spare yourself." When the barbs hurt badly, turn to Shakespeare's Othello: "How poor are they that have not patience! What wound did ever heal but by degrees?"

Dealing with the world outside the gates can also try the patience of us all. Most organizations today want to take their place as esteemed members of their community, to be socially responsible. Financing the local symphony, spearheading a charity drive, or lending managers to a municipal government may satisfy some organizations' social commitment.

Despite such well-motivated efforts, though, there will often be other members of the community who will believe that the local library should have been expanded, scholarships for minorities established, or funds set aside for local mental health projects. These people will believe we missed our "real" social obligation. Managers who did what they thought—and think—was right at the cost of time, energy, and money must be patient when such criticisms arise. Even under such trying circumstances, different voices can be brought together in a harmonious chorus for the benefit of the community, the organizations, and all involved—with patience.

Although organizations have become most responsive to the needs of their community, there are important gaps in performance. For example, have we all done enough to use the full range of talent of the people in our community, no matter how varied or unequal? If not, how can we insist on hiring only the best and yet remain critical of those who are unemployed? Can't we create jobs to use the talents of these people? Do we have the patience to design such jobs, to get the traditionalists among us to accept them, to persuade regulatory agencies to allow such experimentation, and to arrange with our unions for the jobs to be established and staffed? Once again, patience . . . and imagination and commitment.

TAKING TIME

The rush of events against time works against patience. In these days of "time management" and of instant solutions and glib answers, it takes strength and patience to delay, to wait. But if we are to arrive at meaningful plans for the future, we must take the time to argue, to debate, and, ultimately, to reach agreement.

Learning patience results from self-analysis and conscious restraint. But the habit can be formed. The impatience we show by making snap decisions or by "shooting from the hip" is unnecessary—and unwise. So is the impatience we show through sarcasm and anger. A former boss of mine constantly admonished, "Slow down. Slow down. Take time to listen." Have patience. Worthwhile work takes time. [1981]

17   *Reality Is*

Good managers accept the world as it is—for now. Successful managers I have known in both the public and private sectors have this characteristic in common. Those who cannot see or who resist reality—theoreticians and dreamers—rarely achieve major managerial responsibilities, or hold them for long if they do.

Reality *is*. Often it is *now*. Generally it is right *here*. It does not always reflect logic or continuity or consistency with what was, nor does it always make for happiness and contentment. In many instances, if we had a choice, we would not choose reality. But in the short term, few of us have that choice.

POLITICAL REALITIES

A fine sense of reality is important to successful performance in any organizational setting. Many managers interpret this sense of reality to mean an awareness of and responsiveness to the political nature of organizational life. Since all organizations are composed of ambitious people with motives that are sometimes in conflict and sometimes shared, it is inevitable that lobbying and favor swapping will occur and that *ad hoc* coalitions of managers with similar interests will form to further personal and departmental ends.

But there is more to organizational reality than such political machinations. There are organizational rhythms that make some things impossible at one time, yet possible at another. There are long-term and seasonal cycles, terms of office, product life cycles, and recurring deadlines imposed by law, by organizational policy and practice, and by personal commitment.

While present in all organizations, such reality factors are perhaps most pronounced for elected officials. Recently, for example, I heard the mayor of a city describe his experience-based approach to introducing change. "Forget the first and last years or your four-year term if you are a newly elected mayor," he suggested.

Most managers, no matter the nature of their organization, quickly grasp the reality of this advice, but others wonder why such an official should waste the whole first year. It is *not* completely logical, true. But it is a reality of political life.

Managers in all organizations face such realities. The press, for example, is ever present when things go wrong, but where, oh, where is the press in our moments of glory? And what manager has not experienced the disappointment of learning that a talented member of the staff has resigned to move to a new opportunity?

Managers, like most people, dislike conflicts with or between their friends and associates or with outside groups such as consumers or government agencies. In organizations, such conflicts are particularly unpleasant when they occur among top-level executives. But these conflicts are an organizational reality; they are inevitable as long as individuals must try to fit their personal aspirations and desire for recognition with the team's consensus of what the organization's goals should be. And conflicts with outside groups and government agencies are the *modus vivendi* of our time.

On top of all these organizational "facts of life," few managers can escape the reality of the urgencies of day-to-day operations; there is no way to give their ulcers a "break."

HUMAN FALLIBILITY

In a completely different vein, a reality of organizational life today is the delegation of authority and responsibility to lower organizational levels. While policies, standard practices, and the careful selection of those to whom authority is delegated all precede such delegation, this delegation removes many critical decisions from the direct control of higher-level management. As a result, and despite the most conscientious efforts of an organization's top executives, some managers will violate policy, laws, and ethical values. Many of us might wonder how these managers could make such stupid mistakes, but they, after all, are human. But must we destroy a manager's career, or a government official's career, or a clergyman's, because of one well-publicized mistake? Is this truly "reality"? Would it be unreal to apply an appropriate version of the Golden Rule? That human failures will occur is a reality of organizational life. So is the need for some manager to decide whether a reprimand or separation is called for.

Many of these human failures spring from the unremitting pressures of managerial jobs. The survival rate of managers would be much enhanced if such pressures did not exist, if risk were not an inherent aspect of executive work, if the demands of consumers, government, family, stockholders, weather, and the flood of job-related mail would ease. But such a hope is unreal. While a life of blissful somnolence might please some managers, it is not likely to become part of their reality.

There are pleasant realities, too, though. Those with comfortable offices, company airplanes at their disposal, and chauffeured limousines—perquisites designed to facilitate a manager's handling of company business—experience a few of the more enjoyable realities of executive life. But here again these managers are constantly confronted with the barbed criticism of those who view such perquisites as unwarranted luxuries. Is efficiency an unwarranted luxury?

What is, is. Reality is. Managers have little time for jousting with windmills, for belaboring the could-haves, would-haves, or should-haves of their daily lives. They must act in the world as it is. They must decide with the facts as they are. They must see things as clearly, as precisely, and as completely as their ability, the problem, and their time will allow. This is essential if they are to be effective in seizing opportunities or mitigating problems. Managers who are uncomfortable with reality are inefficient decision makers, since they turn away from the facts.

Disappointment . . . Frustration

Some try to excuse their unwillingness to accept things as they are by commenting on their disappointment that things are not as they should be. To fall short of the ideal can legitimately give rise to frustration in a highly motivated manager. And frustration on important goals can reasonably lead to an emotional response. But of what value is such a response? What does it change?

Other managers will deny a reality by rationalizing what they choose not to change—or are unable to change. We have all heard managers defend their rudeness to employees by explaining "they would think you're soft if you give them a kind word." And we have also heard other managers say that it is pointless to try to improve working conditions because employees wouldn't appreciate it if it were done. Do these attitudes reflect reality? Or are they excuses for not wanting to improve things?

All managers who act run risks. But managers who act on the basis of a clear perception of reality run the greatest risks because they are not cloaking their behavior with the shibboleths of the day and the mythology of conventional wisdom. Solving real problems gives opportunities to Monday-morning quarterbacks, the second-guessers. Post mortems have elements of certainty that prescriptions do not. A manager who is a professional takes the risks. He or she wins most, loses some, but always moves on to the next decision with equanimity—and a fine-tuned sense of reality. [1977]

18 A Sense of Humor

Have you read *Parkinson's Law, The Peter Principle, Up the Organization?* These spoofs of management have provided many with some good laughs. Every manager should read them because they are full of situations that he can recognize, people he has known, or glimpses into his own behavior.

Although the nature of humor is frequently misunderstood, humor is actually a sign of maturity because much of it is based on man's recognition of his own humanity. It's an imperative for the manager who realizes that people are his greatest asset. If two people working together are each 5 percent inefficient, the sum of their respective mistakes can easily add up to a solid basis for frustration in their working relationship. But if they maintain a sense of humor about their human failings, these shortcomings can be converted into a long-term asset—a pleasant working relationship that results in achievement through mutual understanding. This means that it is the manager's role to set the stage for an environment where humor can be used constructively.

PROCEDURAL ERRORS

Many individuals find it easy to laugh with errant associates when things go wrong, but a similar mistake made by another department or, worse yet, another organization can be irreconcilable to the same individuals. This is particularly the case with procedural errors stemming from the complex systems of large, departmentalized organizations. Control instruments tend to give managers a false sense of security—but they are man-made and therefore faulty. Imperfect control instruments, both mechanized and procedural, frequently are at the root of petty annoyances that charge those burned with a degree of emotionalism that sometimes borders on irrationality. Picture yourself, for example, in the role of a company president named John Glazer, who recently witnessed one of his factories gutted by a fire. You subscribe to SCOOP MAGAZINE and also advertise in it. Your March issue comes mistakenly addressed to "John Blazer." Can you laugh—or do you cancel all future advertising in the magazine?

NOT SO EXTREME

This may seem like an extreme example, but here is a real one. Recently a letter crossed my desk, stating: "This is the third time I have notified you that the person to whom this notice is going is dead. If you cannot keep track of dead people in your files, certainly you are badly managed, I do not want to belong to an organization like this. I resign."

Because of the name and purpose of our organization, we at AMA tend to get more irate letters than friendly chuckles when our imperfections come to the surface. This is because many people equate *good management* with *perfection*. This is a fallacy. If perfection could be achieved, there would be no need for management at all—and very few opportunities to relax and have a good laugh.   [1971]

PART THREE

A Career

19   *The Excitement of Management*

A successful manager can spend a lifetime on the job without encountering more than just a transitory perfect match between management theory and management in practice. Only inexperienced managers expect the application of perfect management theory to result in a perfect organization. Actually, even the best management organizations are flawed, even though they are essentially healthy.

That is not to say that it's safe to ignore for very long even one flaw, however minor, in the organization structure. All manifestations of weakness should be treated and, if they can't be cured immediately, checked repeatedly and kept under control.

Somerset Maugham once wrote that perfection is "nothing more than a complete adaptation to the environment; but the environment is constantly changing, so perfection can never be more than transitory." Living with weaknesses of a minor nature is acceptable to good managements; they worry, raise alarms, and implement new approaches and techniques primarily when problems are deeprooted and threaten the organization's future stability and success.

An Organizational Snapshot

If it were possible to freeze an organization on a given day, we could identify the various management beliefs, theories, and practices to which its managers subscribe. But changes would begin to occur the very next day. Economics, politics, and daily competition inevitably influence management behavior in even the smallest organization. Research and continuing education undoubtedly alter practices and styles. On the surface an organization may appear as the epitome of a distinguishing management technique; beneath this highly visible mantle, however, simmers a potpourri of management styles and concepts that its managers have adopted to accommodate to, or to control, the daily operational stresses and strains with which they must contend.

Let us suppose that all the managers in a company follow one management philosophy. Realistically, of course, this is impossible—just as it is impossible to freeze an organization. Nevertheless, we can speculate that an entire company's management believes in decentralized, bottom-line-oriented, incentive-laden jobs as the basis for success. A month later, chances are that some of the original group will have changed jobs within the organization or left for outside positions. The newcomers who replace them might subscribe to everything except decentralization, believing that tight control exercised by centralized management is more likely to achieve the best results.

SOURCES OF TURMOIL

This one philosophical and structural change can cause turmoil within a company:

- If the change involves a president or a vice-president, all the other managers in the organization will have to alter their styles and approaches to problems.
- If the change involves middle managers, who play a vital role as liaison between upper management and the firm's line workers, a new communications network will have to be established.
- If new people are introduced at the bottom of the structure, a certain amount of chaos can be expected, and even customers may be negatively affected for a while.

And yet, an outsider—a consultant, say, called in to assess the health and needs of the organization—would not necessarily see cause for alarm: What appear to many to be major disruptions within the organization are most likely the symptoms of a normal organization experiencing change.

Not everyone recognizes such changes as a normal manifestation of organizational development, however. But those who do correctly assess the thrust of internal turmoil gain an insightful perspective on the hiring, promotions, and transfers . . . and see the true dimension of the overall shift in organization structure and operational direction.

In these days of widespread organizational turmoil—the drive for higher productivity, the pressing needs of minority groups, the demand for bottom-up participation and self-expression—many managers are looking for quick antidotes to disconcerting problems. As a result, many theories of management are being offered as approaches to resolving these conflicts. Taken one at a time they seem plausible. But even if all the theories of management were compatible—and they are not—individuals are so arrayed in organizations that what may work for one group may send another into complete disarray. The theories that research has demonstrated so well in defined situations may not be fully compatible until their advocates have worked together for years.

Why this incompatibility exists should be obvious. In any organization, only a few managers are likely to have studied a particular theory endorsed by one executive. Many develop their own pragmatic formulas out of experience. And among those who have formally studied management techniques, two groups usually emerge—those who have adopted or developed a comprehensive theory of management, and others who have selectively mastered segments of theory or are well acquainted with certain practices that, in their experience at least, have been shown to "work."

To the inexperienced observer—or manager—such dichotomies may spell trouble, at least in the short run, and an off-the-cuff diagnosis may conclude that, indeed, something is wrong. But Albert Einstein's observation that "perfection of means and confusion of goals seem . . . to characterize our age" has pertinence to organizational dynamics as well. Criticisms of organizational performance should be investigated, but it is careless to assume that discontent generated by managerial approaches to problems means a doomsday situation exists.

In fact, a good manager knows he or she is dealing with something less than perfection. But detouring around potholes does not mean that the good manager is ignoring a problem. After all, a squeaky fender doesn't necessarily mean the automobile is falling apart; you note the problem and get it fixed. But don't be surprised if the car gets a flat tire tomorrow.

Well-meaning, but misinformed, organization critics sometimes advocate issuance of a top-management mandate that certain "good management" practices be followed under threat of penalties for those who would deviate. At the same time they may applaud decentralization because it promotes creativity and self-realization. They sense no contradiction in these positions, but good management will automatically adjust.

THE EXCITEMENT OF MANAGEMENT

Some executives believe that a companywide sense of job satisfaction is a reliable index of good management. Other managers prefer to measure managerial performance by the results achieved on the ever-visible bottom line. Balancing these approaches to organizational diagnosis is not easy, because they do not necessarily operate in a cause-effect relationship.

A paucity of data showing a relationship between job satisfaction and productivity may upset those who find comfort in believing there should be such a relationship. For example, efforts to enforce tight job definitions and tying of rewards to the achievement of rigidly defined standards of performance invite criticism as threats to job satisfaction. But as good managers in any organization know, some jobs should be threatened, and criticism of such performance criteria may well indicate that some organizational sore spots need treatment.

We try to make management decisions that, if everything goes right, will preclude future problems. But everything does not always go right, and managers therefore must be problem solvers as well as decision makers.

These opportunities for action generate the excitement of management.   [1981]

20   *By Whose Authority?*

It's not easy these days to find an effective manager who admits to running his or her unit, section, division, or company on an authoritarian basis. If their authority is challenged, good managers usually can assert with confidence that "I am the boss" and take appropriate action on their own initiative. But chances are they are keenly aware of the crucial difference between "authority" and "authoritarianism," and most tend to shy from the authoritarian label that so many of yesterday's managers adopted routinely.

This bellwether stance in managerial attitudes has developed gradually over a period of about 25 years; it emerged under the influence of theories espoused by organization and behavioral scientists who studied why certain managerial techniques and styles appeared to work in some situations but not in others. Thus managers who have adopted a style, or combination of styles, emphasizing participative or consultative techniques now tend to reject the authoritarian posture. When confronted by the humanistic requirements of the participative management format, would-be authoritarians often become uneasy about imposing their will without some sort of prior strategic consultation.

THE GOOD OLD DAYS

This is not to say, however, that there are no managers who, yearning perhaps for the "good old days," point to their success on the bottom line and reason that their method of managing works, whatever name you put on it. They insist that the end—the bottom line—justifies the means, and they do not worry about how you label the means.

Over the years I have seen thousands of managers learning,

69

discussing, and sharing their experiences. It is impossible to find a universal reaction to any management theory, but certain patterns do emerge. For example, we can point to top managers who followed an authoritarian style on their way to the top, then switched to more participative techniques at the height of their success. Among middle managers, a typical behavior is to advocate more participatory practices, particularly in reaction to an authoritarian boss; later, however, it is not unusual to see many of these same managers, anxious to ensure success in their own jobs, leaning to authoritarian measures in their relationships with subordinates.

And how about the young graduates who become unqualified boors on their first managerial job despite their heavy, recent classroom saturation in management theory? Their overenthusiastic desire to impress on everyone in the vicinity just who is the boss frequently generates authoritarian behavior that, on the surface at least, appears to accomplish the job in far less time than a participatory technique would require.

The situation of the moment also is a factor in decisions on what kind of managerial technique should be applied at a given time. But it is incorrect to contend that all elements in a situation must be favorable to ensure successful results. In his recent book, *Leadership* (AMACOM, 1981), which focuses on strategies for organizational effectiveness, Prof. James J. Cribbin argues that all managerial leadership is situational and that the situation is a necessary arena in which the leader must operate. He states:

> To a considerable extent it can make or break the leader, but to attribute too much to the situation is a mistake. It's better to think of the matter as a pair of scissors. One blade represents what the leaders bring to the situation—their philosophy, education, experience, talents, competence, skills, attitudes, and so on. The other blade represents the situation that provides the leaders with both constraints and opportunities. The skill resides not in the situations but in the managers' deftness at making their behavior congruent with the realities.

In defining the limits of effective managerial leadership, it is easy to confuse the concepts of authority with those of power. Authority is the right of the individual or group to secure compliance from others in order to carry out specific activities. It permits the use of certain rewards and penalties to accomplish this objective. It is a privilege that is granted, but when used beyond the specific organizational requirements of a job or a clear statement of objectives, it loses its positive thrust, thereby opening the door to authoritarianism in all its negative aspects.

In contrast to authority, power is a force that must be grasped. When a manager can reward and punish to bring about a desired end, he has established a power source. In his book *The Management Process*, Dr. William Fox describes the reach of power this way:

> Formal authority does not give a superior the right to make someone do something in any absolute sense, but it does provide important penalties and rewards in the form of promotions, job assignments, pay increases, and so on, which give him a very real measure of power over his subordinates.

This "reward and coercion" base of power, as it has been termed, provides managers a highly effective tool, but it must be used wisely. Quickness to discipline and slowness to reward can quickly turn legitimate power into authoritarianism.

ADHERING TO STANDARDS

A manager also runs the risk of overstepping authority and embracing authoritarianism, willingly or not, when he fails to plan, set proper job standards, or clearly establish work rules before assigning people to the specific jobs. Managers who trade on title rather than specific accountabilities are probably authoritarian types no matter what techniques they use in managing a project.

The word authority derives from a Latin root meaning to "increase." It is aptly used when applied to a situation where a manager is growing in expertise by listening to his superiors, peers, and subordinates, by understanding key situations, and by helping those who are trying to complete a task. The concept of authority advances to still another level when "authority" is personalized—that is, when someone is described as "an authority" in a specific field or discipline.

The positive connotation of authority begins to turn sour, however, when the manager who holds authority doesn't manage positively and does not see his or her job as helping others to grow and to be successful.

Since the proper use of authority is a key element in the effective use of participatory techniques to attain managerial goals, any warning that authority can be quickly channeled into authoritarianism may sound to some like a warning against participation. Not at all. Managers should be aware, however, that participation is not necessarily the opposite of authoritarianism.

One of the great myths of organizational leadership, says Professor Cribbin, is that you must be democratic. "Participatory democracy is excellent," he writes, "if it does not degenerate into a popularity contest and if it results in better courses of action." Warning against the "wet finger" approach to leadership—"whichever way the wind blows, the manager bends"—he wonders about "managers who are reluctant to take a lonely position based on convictions when such a posture is called for."

Indeed, some managers use participation as a manipulative process. Others see it as an opportunity to escape responsibility. And if a group participates in a decision that the manager accepts even though he believes it is wrong, what is the position of a manager from an accountability point of view? Has he not conceded to a process rather than a good result? Again, how is this person different from the bottom-line-oriented authoritarian? Letting the group dominate is an easy way for a weak leader to avoid responsibility.

Effective managers thrive on authority not because it permits them per se to impose their will on others but because it opens doors to the sources of power that, if wielded effectively, permit the organization and its members to participate productively and enjoyably in its growth and rewards.   [1982]

21   *Don't Fret, Look Ahead*

Pilots don't use rearview mirrors. What is ahead is so critical and happening so fast they have little time to be concerned about what is behind. Wind, speed, checkpoints, destination, fuel, direction—right now—these are the critically important matters to which a pilot *must* attend. He may wish he had not run into turbulence or encountered headwinds, but if he did, it's a fact, it's past, it's relevant only through its effects on the future. To fret over what could have been, or should have been, steals valuable time from the critical decisions at hand.

Dynamic managers are so intent on the future that they, too, accept the past. There are those who accuse managers of being callous and insensitive to the effects of their actions because they do not do enough public penance for their "sins." While there is no doubt that public—and private—penance is good for the charac-ter—and the soul—my experience is that managers regret their mistakes and errors just as much as any other *human* being. I have heard foremen tell how miserable they felt when they dismissed an ineffective worker, even when they had full justification for their action. I have sat on boards of directors of companies that have had product failures where the failure produced, not just an outspoken consumer reaction, but also a depressing sense of failure in a group of top executives.

WHAT'S DONE IS DONE

Managers are not callous, they are realistic. What is done is done. While we may be able to reconstruct and reinterpret the past, we cannot undo events that have already occurred. Realizing this, effective managers have learned that their opportunities exist in the

73

future; they have also learned how to switch quickly to the future in their thinking and their actions. They are not indifferent to the past; they only appear to be. The failures of the past are a powerful teacher. Most managers learn quickly from this unwelcome teacher and then go on from there.

Effective managers live in the present—but concentrate on the future. They accept their responsibility to make things happen. Managers are the force that brings change and correction. Consumerism is a great case in point.

Managers don't deny the validity of the consumer's right to honest and fair dealing and to a product that is safe and dependable and manufactured as specified. After all, managers and their families are consumers too, and as such, they have the same expectations as other consumers. But the actions that have come from the consumer movement—government regulations, investigations of human and mechanical failures, court cases, constantly increasing social pressures—all have heavy overtones of the past because they have usually arisen out of past events. Such actions and events are usually studied by managers for the lessons to be learned and to obtain bench marks to gauge the future. That done, however, these managers advance.

MANAGERS MOVE AHEAD

Managers' emphasis on the future and reluctance to dwell in the past explains, in part, at least, their irritation with the media. Since most news focuses on past events, newspapers, television, and radio use the past to create their products—today. Managers who have already learned from the past and who have moved into the future have little patience for such retrospective ruminations.

The manager who dwells on the past is like the automobile driver who is so intent on watching out of the rearview mirror that he makes those who ride with him uneasy because he is not watching the road. A switch in concentration from the future to the past is a definite sign of executive "senility." If any manager at any level tells you "I can remember when . . ." or "The way it used to be is . . ." or "Did I tell you about the time I . . ." or "Let me tell you how workers behaved during the Depression . . . ," I assure you that managerial senility has set in, no matter how healthy the individual may look. A manager who has turned his attention to the past is like the driver who spends more time looking behind than looking ahead, a real menace to all those who "travel" with him.

LOOKING BACKWARD

This looking backwards can take place at any age. Some professors end their lives of active, productive research when they are awarded their Ph.D.'s, and life thereafter focuses on recalling what they discovered in their doctoral research. How sad that they relegate themselves to the daydreams of the unproductive rather than to the joy of a continual unfolding and development of their creative talents and their knowledge. So, too, for the middle managers who rest on past glories and the seeming security of entrenched positions. They guard the gates of their present preserve, and by turning their backs on opportunities to advance or to try new jobs, they miss the rebirth that comes with new challenges. To be challenged is to incur the risk that you may fail, and this element of risk is what frightens many managers in mid-career.

Some young people, too, turn their backs on risky undertakings. This is most unfortunate since the time to experiment is before assuming heavy personal responsibilities. Young people have more future than past, and the temptation to look back should not be so intense, of course. But some still do, and it is such a waste. Most young people, however, do look ahead, and their strength can be judged by how enthusiastically they move into the future rather than remain in the present.

The Ancient Mariner of management may have a word of wisdom at the end of his story, but he can use up so much valuable time holding you with his "skinny hand" and "glittering eye." There is always something to be learned from those with experience, but the good manager needs all the time available to help him prepare for and make the future. Wisdom is not an albatross of inapplicable experience; it is not something to be collected, like memories; it is something to be used.

"WE ARE HERE TODAY"

Managers generally have more plans and ambitions than they can ever realize. If they don't, they should. Recently I heard a president say to a group, "Where we should be heading ten years from now is. . . ." A vice-president interrupted him to say, "Harry, you and I won't be here ten years from now." Harry shot back with some irritation. "That's not the point. The future starts with today's decisions, and we *are* here today."

How often managers forget the simple truth that the future will be made by today's decisions. Future plans start with today's decisions. But an objective on which action cannot or will not begin until sometime in the future is not a valid present objective. The essence of planning is the futurity of present decisions—and actions. An art of management is to use today's decisions to create in managers a commitment to future objectives.

In the past week I met a president who is 73 years of age and who is talking excitedly about the possible technical breakthroughs his company can make in the next ten years. Shortly after that meeting, I met another, younger man, 45 years of age, who gave me the glorious history of his company and told me how discouraged he is by government regulation, consumerism, and unions. He wants to retire at 55. He should.   [1977]

22 *Executive Boredom*

Mature executives don't get bored. They have the commitment to a vision of the future of their organizations that keeps them enthusiastically engaged in their jobs day after long, hard day.

To be sure, some managers may get bored with their jobs. Perhaps even some CEOs lose their zest for their work. A distinguished president of a not-for-profit organization, for example, declared recently that a top executive is good for only seven to ten years in his or her job. As this president analyzes top-executive job performance, the first two years an executive spends on a job are invested in getting acquainted with the organization and deciding what needs to be done; the next two to three years are given to implementing this program; and thereafter, having done for the organization whatever he or she could, the executive finds the job becomes more or less repetitive—and boring. For this president, ten years is as long as any CEO can stay in the office and off the golf course during the workday.

This attitude is ridiculous. That some very good people have accepted it doesn't make it right—or understandable. Perhaps what they mean is that the organization has become bored with the executive because he or she lacks enthusiasm and spontaneity. Or perhaps it is a matter of the CEO or other executive becoming so predictable that the tension has gone out of his relationship with his organization.

Effective managers must be predictable and unpredictable in turn—at the right times and for the right things. For those actions and decisions that relate closely to a subordinate's feelings of security, that define for him or her what is to be done on the job and how well, the supervisor should be predictable, consistent. But for many other actions and decisions, a healthy dose of unpredictability can keep the organization just enough on edge to make each day interesting. It's like a wife greeting her husband at the door with a new dress and hairdo on an evening with nothing special scheduled; he has to wonder what in the world is going on, and with that wonder there would be just a touch of excitement.

NEEDED: A VISION OF THE FUTURE

Poor management can also lead to a bored organization. Inadequate long-term planning, for example, seems to correlate with a lack of organizational zest.

Even today some managers do not believe in long-term planning. If management is an *ad hoc* adventure with only modest and not very challenging incremental changes each year, boredom can set in early. But when the leaders of an organization believe in taking a long view, when they have a vision of where the organization is going and of what it can become, excitement follows.

Inspiring leaders have dreams. They may know they will not live long enough to see their dreams come true, but nevertheless they strive constantly to realize their vision of what might be. They are always busy because they have so many things they want to do before they retire—or die. For example, a young man I knew found out during a hospital stay that he had terminal cancer. After being told, he asked for a dictating machine; he wanted to write a book. This was something he had wanted to do, and he now realized that his time was running out. He finished the book before he died. It was an excellent little book of meditations for young clerics, a fine piece of work. This outstanding young man lived life fully to the very end because he had dreams.

A LACK OF FOCUS FOR SELF-DEVELOPMENT

Managers who become immersed in routine, who do nothing more than visit the same old customers each day, who plod about the laboratory, who tour the hospital, who watch the customers in the bank, can quite easily get bored. Routine tasks *are* boring. But good managers are creative—and long-term planners.

Managers who do not adopt planning as an everyday process may fall behind in their knowledge and skill. The organization and their jobs pass them by, and they soon become physically and mentally tired. Lacking a plan for the future, their self-development efforts lack direction and focus, and the state of the management art in fields that are important to their futures advances much more rapidly than their own knowledge and skill. The demands of their jobs increase, but their skills decrease. While young these managers may have been outstanding, but at the threshold of what should be their most productive years, they are barely adequate.

That jobs grow, and undoubtedly will continue to grow, in their demands should be obvious to all who work. Even the most prosaic jobs are affected by the day-by-day impact of technical innovations.

In years past, for example, all that was required of a home

handyman was that he know how to use a screwdriver. How times have changed! With the complexity of modern household equipment, repairs to even the simplest gadget require almost an engineering degree.

Needless to say, the professions are experiencing the same explosion of knowledge and change. Imagine an accountant who ignores the rulings of the IRS or the Financial Accounting Standards Board, and think of the dentist who has more dials and switches on her equipment than the pilot of a small plane. Even art takes new forms. And colleges are giving courses in recreation.

Such changes should not be surprising. Neither should the increasing rate of change. A competitive economic system pushes improvement as a way of life. And even in socialistic societies, where the rate of innovation once seemed slower, change is spurred by the challenge of meeting or exceeding the achievements of capitalistic countries.

Only the completely withdrawn could be bored in such a world.

Most people, of course, do grow in competence. Some growth comes from additional formal education; most growth, however, comes from informal special training and on-the-job experience. Association with able people stimulates growth, particularly if we are able to maintain adequate relationships with them. Most research has, in fact, indicated that this kind of on-the-job coaching and experience is the *sine qua non* of effective management development.

Unfortunately, many people who receive outstanding formal educations lose in the process the ability to learn from others. Perhaps what they have really lost is the ability to empathize with people, most importantly, with their subordinates. Perhaps, too, this weakness could be overcome if college graduates started in industry as workers making or selling the product. If managers experienced the work lives of their subordinates, they might understand and empathize with them better. Some highly intelligent college graduates do empathize with their associates, of course, but some never sense the way life is in the shop, at the counter, at the switchboard, or at a routine desk job.

Outstanding managers seem to mature quickly in their skill in personal relationships. Experienced managers recognize this ability as one mark of effective leadership. Effective leaders display empathy for the least significant person in the organization and match this empathy with recognition and appreciation.

ONE MANAGER'S CAREER

The figure below diagrams what often happens to promising managers and shows what may be any manager's problem tomorrow— for himself or for someone who reports to him. Points A and B depict a young manager's capacity vis-à-vis the demands of his job at the time of hire. The figure is obviously for an outstanding manager: His capacity far exceeds the demands of the job. As a result, the company is comfortable and pleased with its new manager's performance.

In the figure, the line *AD* represents the growth in the state of the art. (A graph showing exponential growth would undoubtedly be more accurate.) Compare the slope of line *BC* with that of *AD*. Job demands have grown much faster than this manager has grown in competence. If the performance appraisal system is at all sensitive, this narrowing of the gap between job demands and managerial competence will show in appraisals that move from outstanding to marginal.

What is such a manager's supervisor to do? If the supervisor is typical, he or she will attribute the lower appraisals to preoccupation with family concerns—or maturation. These explanations may be partially true, but none suggests a curative. If the person has been promoted a few times, his new supervisors will wonder how his earlier supervisors could have been so wrong about the manager. The problem, of course, is that no one took the trouble to forecast developmental requirements for the person if he was to continue as an outstanding performer—his obligation to himself and his organization.

DEVELOPMENT IS A PERSONAL PROBLEM

Line *BE* suggests the development potential of the individual, what could have been achieved if he had been alerted to the need and given assistance. Development, of course, is not entirely a company matter. Development is each manager's personal problem—opportunity—and an opportunity that a manager and company should address together very early in a manager's career.

Since most development is self-development, a company's efforts in this regard can only supplement a manager's efforts; they cannot supplant them. Many companies and managers mistakenly believe that organizations have the obligation to furnish developmental assistance for their people. No, at best the organization can provide only a few opportunities for growth; the individual, in his or her application to the work at hand, provides most of the opportunities. Interestingly, though, the personnel records of most companies list only company development efforts.

For company and manager, *X* is the critical point. At *X* the manager has become a marginal employee. At this point it is almost too late to take corrective action; it is almost too late for the last years of the manager's career to be as rich and rewarding as the early years. If the lines representing job demands and competence cross, the manager will be spending his last years in the demeaning role of a "hanger on." Rather than ending his career with the independence and pride of an outstanding contributor, the manager sneaks to the retirement line—a ward of the company.

Why does this so often happen to managers between the ages of 55 and 60? Perhaps it is that their initially very good performance caused them and their supervisors to be insensitive to the rapidly rising *AD* line. Strong basic preparation and initial performance carry managers through many years on a new job without substantial challenge. By the time the manager and his supervisor realize what has happened, the shortcomings in performance are a result of years of neglected development. Development must start early and be continuous; just imagine trying to learn all about electronics in a year or two.

A Lag in Self-Image

It is hard to forget or correct the self-images of the past. To the person who was a star at 30 it is hard to see himself as a has-been at 55.

Some people, of course, do feel themselves slipping. They can feel the world and the organizations in which they are working moving faster than they are and, very wisely, they take early retirement. And sometimes, of course, a supervisor or the board will step in and say, "Look, you're not doing your job and we must do something about you." As a matter of fact, this is where a good board is very important. It is the board's responsibility to evaluate the CEO, and the CEO sets the tone of the organization. But managers at all levels must face up to this problem, regardless of the tone or climate at the top.

Even if a manager's supervisor doesn't take the initiative and tell him where he's falling down, his subordinates usually will. It may not come directly. That's a hard, a risky, thing for a subordinate to do. But subordinates will drop many clues: "Jim, let me explain this to you." Translated this means, "Look, you dummy, you don't understand what's going on anymore. Let me catch you up with what has been happening over the past three or four years." They will say, "Just let me explain that in a little more detail." Your subordinates will use such throwaway phrases to tell you that the state of the management art is passing you by.

In theory an organization's performance appraisal system should pick up those managers who are coasting or who have gone into early retirement on the job. In fact, however, we appraise so poorly that appraisals are of little help. With a good appraisal system we would be measuring a manager's performance against established standards of performance and so would know early when the manager was slipping.

But we don't do this. Few companies have well-developed standards of performance and few managers seem to have the stomach for leveling with their subordinates. What happens instead is that each performance review is a pleasant social occasion with little that is critical or substantial communicated to the employee. Suddenly one day a hard decision must be made, and the employee who was just a happy visit once a year becomes a problem to be handled. It is difficult, though, to confront someone who has for so long thought everything was going well with the judgment that he has suddenly become a marginal performer at best, and more probably a nonperformer, in any hard measurement of his results. This is the high price of managerial weakness.

Such ineffective managerial performance can be overcome with relative ease if companies invest in developing standards of performance. When standards of performance exist, a manager is not dependent on what someone else tells him about his performance; he can judge for himself. He knows when he is doing his job because he has an impersonal, always-present frame of reference within which to judge how well he is doing. Standards of performance are clear, objective, and public. It's like golf. Everyone knows what par is for each hole and for the course; it's published on the scorecard. Even a person who is playing a course for the first time can rate his performance: All he has to do is compare his score with par. If a score is far off par, the golfer knows that more practice or lessons are needed. If a score is at par or below, things are obviously going well. If you have a ruler, you don't need others to tell you the length of the cloth.

SOMETIMES ORGANIZATIONS FAIL

Now sometimes a manager may be spinning his wheels through no fault of his own. His organization may not be giving him the resources he needs to do his job. After a reasonable effort has been made, if nothing changes, there is little point in fighting a losing battle. Talents like muscles grow with use. If a manager is in a situation that does not tax his talents, and hence stifles his growth, it is usually better for him to leave.

People in political life have learned to resign. Able people in government will often become ineffective, not because of any lessening of their talent, but because of differences in their policy orientation—or in their political sponsorship and constituency—from those in policy-level positions. In such situations, they forthrightly resign—with honor.

In many organizations, however, the word "resignation" has taken on overtones of deception and misrepresentation. Most people in business, for example, assume that people don't resign, they are fired—but are given the opportunity to resign to put a good face on it. How sad! I think there are times in all organizations for able but not fully used people to leave. Sometimes these people have grown beyond their jobs and the organization cannot provide opportunities that are challenging to them. In other cases, people have developed new values as they have matured, values that can no longer be fully realized in their present organization. Certainly, in such situations, to leave is preferable to a slow decline in talents through disuse and to the frustration in values denied.

BOREDOM IS A SYMPTOM

Boredom in business? Boredom for CEOs? Yes, boredom can occur, but when it does, it is a symptom of more fundamental problems.

The organization may be bored with its managers and their lack of spontaneity and verve. These managers may also not be committed to an exciting vision of what they and their organizations can become in the future. But perhaps even more important, the organization may not challenge these managers through demanding standards of performance. In any case, and regardless of the reasons, when a mature and able manager feels bored, he should seriously consider changing jobs, changing companies—or simply retiring. It is not fair to anyone for half a leader to hold a full-time leadership job.   [1978]

23   *The Present Power of Hope*

A small community I once knew lies now at the bottom of a lake. An old man who had lived there now operates a fine restaurant on a hillside overlooking the lake shore. When I visited his place recently, he told me an intriguing story about how the community, once a picturesque little village, responded to the news that its homes and businesses would be sacrificed to make way for a flood control project.

Local business leaders led the battle to reverse the decision, first seeking political aid, then taking their case into court. But it was a losing battle; flood control needs down stream prevailed.

The community soon began to waste away. Saddened and disheartened, the business leaders let their properties decline; indeed, the entire village seemed to crumble, and when I knew the place, the common opinion was that the lake would conceal an eyesore. The only people who visited the area went there only to eat at the neat little diner in the middle of town. Its cheery atmosphere and good food reflected the optimisim of the owner, who nonetheless became the butt of jokes of the community's other businessmen because he continued to work so hard. How they laughed when he decided to open a fancier "branch" on the hill behind the village to accommodate the patrons who drove in from miles around to enjoy his good food.

I am sure you are miles ahead of me at this point. When the flood control project was finished, guess who had the first and only attractive restaurant on the edge of the newly constructed lake.

FROM PRESENT TO FUTURE

The old man, the owner, told me his success story when I asked him about a sign that hung on the wall of his restaurant's waiting lounge. It read: "Where there is no hope in the future there is no power in the present."

"That sign hung behind the cash register in my diner," the man said. "Many who saw it recognized it as a wise saying, but few knew what it meant to me. Do you think I would have poured cash into keeping up that diner if I didn't hope for this place I have now?"

He pointed out that anyone could have found out where the water's edge was to be by asking the Corps of Engineers. But the others in the village wanted only the present; they couldn't see the future. "They became fatalists and lazy," the restaurant owner said.

The word "hope" is one we often throw away. "I hope you make it. . . . I hope you are successful." But it can be more than just an idle good wish. It represents strong desire or anticipation of something in the future and suggests insights into how that future is going to be achieved.

In its best sense, hope is basic to good planning both for organizations and for individuals. Well-defined plans make a manager's decisions easier, more precise, easier to execute. And to focus on a matter of specific current interest, consider its manifestation in career planning. If linked to hope, a career can fulfill Karl Menninger's description of "an adventure, a going forward—a confident search for a rewarding life."

For some, however, career planning is only a succession of jobs, each a bit better than the last. For many, just getting a job is a great accomplishment. But we live in a country where education and economic opportunity inspire the best talent to hope for more than a job. We often do not know where that talent lies until a career is well under way.

POWER OF THE MANAGER

Managers play an important role in generating the "power" of a current job performance that leads to a career. The manager who impedes an individual's future or who, regretting the present, does not fortify the hope of younger people contributes to costly turnover. Poor managers produce workers who, in their bankruptcy of hope, can't wait for retirement or a second career. Good managers are more likely to have workers whose hopes have been fulfilled, who can't understand why they must retire.

Career planning, like so many other managerial movements, tends to get very theoretical. Sometimes it is divorced from on-the-spot management and operates as part of personnel or the human resources function. In high schools it may be offered as a kind of extra staff service handled by nonteaching guidance counselors. But we often have managers and teachers who feel they have enough to do without hand-holding adults. Fulfillment of a career based on the strength of current performance is nonetheless so dependent upon the chain of managers or teachers that any other approach is close to a waste of money. Which of us can think through how another life should be pathed? We can evaluate performance, but how do we analyze another's hope?

THE BIG SWITCH

Years ago a vice-president of personnel told how, with a Ph.D. in physics from a top university, he moved into his present job. Spurred by a hope to be a pioneer in nuclear technology, he landed a job with a top company and within five years was named head of its nuclear section where one of his responsibilities was the training of young technicians. Before then he had never known the excitement of watching people grow, and fascinated by the experience, he eventually sought and obtained the job of training director of the company. The switch changed everything he had ever dreamed of, and eventually he moved into the top personnel position.

How many teachers, managers, personnel counselors, and psychologists have expressed disappointment with this man because he "never achieved his great potential?" All I know is that one man who helped him switch from physics to personnel is proud, and his wife is happy with his success in fulfilling a hope he redirected early in his career.

THE CONTINUITY OF HOPE

The continuity in a person's life is so personal it can be easily ignored by the series of managers who, knowingly or not, help shape careers. If the managers in a person's career are not oriented to his or her hopes, however flexible, and are insensitive to the power that good counseling can provide, then career planning offers only a modest exercise from which little can be expected. If it is to work, career planning must be a total company dedication.

Lateral movement for general management is not easy. Moving a sales manager into finance can be resisted with the easy question, "What does he/she know about finance?" Teaching fundamentals is not always easy. It is easier to let someone outside the company do it. More than knowledge is involved. Decision making in finance— or any other function—goes beyond knowledge limits and requires a broad sensitivity to the total environment in which such decisions are made.

My friend at the lakeside restaurant knew, perhaps intuitively, that power in the present lies in the quality of decisions people make. And he made his confident in the hope that he wanted more than just a village diner in his future. Other present power elements are willingness to take constructive criticism if it leads to growth, readiness for challenging new assignments, and quickness in recovering from failure. It seems he also passed those tests. And as should any good manager, the restaurant owner knew these facets of organizational planning—of personal career planning—as well.

Managers have a responsibility for the careers of others as well as their own. They can strongly influence performance and success of others on the job.

As a managerial technique or device, career planning is only in its beginnings. But it is the key to the future of most organizations. Will managers push to make it successful? We hope so. [1980]

24   *Preparing Future Leaders*

The president of your company in the year 2005 is working some-where—right now. So are the rest of his or her top-management group. But none of these managers may make it to those jobs without planned preparation, and 24 years is not much time.

Many things about the future are unknown and unknowable. But we do know about the people who will be staffing the top levels of our organizations then. With few exceptions, those who will be our leaders in 2005 are out of college and working in their first jobs. They may be working for us—or with us. If they are working for us, we will influence the next 40 years or more of their lives and through them the future of our organization. Directly and indi-rectly, by our behavior, our attitudes, our values, we will mold and shape them day by day.

THIS EAGER BREED

Evidence suggests that these talented young people are an excep-tional group. Eager for responsibility, well prepared, these begin-ning managers are as hard working and socially dedicated as any of their forebears—if not more so. In this talent pool are the entrepre-neurs, the scientists, the leaders of the future. And the organiza-tion—and country—that nurtures them will have a future.

Aristotle said that young people "have exalted notions because they have not yet been humbled by life or learned its necessary limitations." How fortunate! This is the very spirit of youth, and this spirit is what gives the young the verve to say "can do."

Rarely will these young managers give their supervisors the respect these older managers think they deserve. Young managers "know all the answers" even before they have walked the course. Again, good! Wise older managers don't really mind the challenges of the young. They have the satisfaction of their accomplishments; they have had their successes. Often as young managers they were just as "disrespectful" of their supervisors as their juniors are today. But along with their "disrespect" they had the instinct of success, the touch of leadership. If they reflect, they will remember, too, that it was a respected manager who coached them and guided them to the right path and to the habit of effectiveness. With these managers as their mentors, they listened, they imitated, they learned—and they grew.

Young managers come to their jobs today better educated than any previous generation of managers. But if we look behind the degree, we find not managers but accountants, financial managers, marketers, human resources managers, psychologists, lawyers, engineers, physicists, chemists, and other specialists. Where are the managers? The generalists? Few, if any, of this eager breed have been prepared for management jobs as such. And those few who have studied "management" know it only in theory, not in practice. Effective management is not a theory, it is artful performance.

Artful performance is the kind of performance that we hear in an accomplished string quartet, or see on the stage in a well-rehearsed ballet or in the theater on a brilliant opening night. Makarova practiced for many, many years developing her art. Sir Laurence served his long apprenticeship, too. And Menuhin spent hours after countless hours perfecting his technique. Practice, practice, practice. This is the secret of artful performance in the performing arts, and it is no less the secret in the art of management.

To be effective in management requires practice in perfecting necessary skill. Present-day education does not provide these skills, and it probably should not. Education should be directed to developing the values, the attitudes, the ethics of the manager, not his or her skills. These values, attitudes, and ethical concerns are critical to effective management, but not sufficient for it. It takes years of practice to become adept at resolving conflicts, in negotiating agreements, in speaking before groups, and in counseling subordinates, to pick only a few of the many skills of management. The young manager who is not encouraged to practice these skills in his first management assignment, albeit managing only ten employees, will not be able to exercise these skills should he ever become responsible for 100 or 1,000 employees. Indeed, lacking these skills, he or she may never be given such a larger responsibility.

THE FIRST JOB

All the skills of management can be practiced in the first-level management job. Such jobs provide a laboratory for experimentation and practice. Mistakes will occur; indeed, they are inevitable. Fortunate is the young manager who has a boss who teaches the "art" of management by sensitive coaching and constructive counseling when mistakes occur—or sometimes overlooks the mistakes completely. A climate of acceptance and support reduces the tension in those who are trying hard to succeed. A mistake properly handled is a learning opportunity that ensures that the young manager will give an artful performance the next time and the next and the next, each time with less effort than the last. And from such successes comes confidence.

In beginning managerial jobs, decisions are limited in impact and generally short in time span. With each higher-level job, the impact becomes greater and the time span longer. And the larger the organization, the greater the impact and the longer the time span.

By the year 2005 the management leader will be working in a larger "world" and thinking in terms of more people, more dollars— or yen or deutsche marks—and longer time spans. He or she will be a long-term planner—by necessity. But a manager doesn't learn suddenly how to make decisions when confronted for the first time with the need to decide in situations of uncertainty and ambiguity. Decision making is a learned skill. Practice in making decisions should begin as soon as possible for young managers. But decision making for only short-term planning is inadequate preparation because it is only a small part of shaping the long-term picture. Leaps of thought and discontinuities are the milieu of the long-term planner. The long-term planner's attitude is, "It wasn't raining when Noah built the ark."

PRACTICE, PRACTICE, PRACTICE

Senior-level managers increasingly must present their views to groups and the media. How do they learn to do this? Is this a skill that flowers suddenly when needed? Unlikely. It is rather a skill that is developed by painstaking practice over many, many years. Successful managers are competent speakers. "Leaders" who are inarticulate on the platform or television make us all uneasy, and serve us poorly. Why, we ask, are those who espouse "radical" causes so clever with words and in debate? The chances are that they have been speaking for years—practicing, if you will—and are now comfortable before groups and able to think on their feet.

By the year 2005 managers will have to be able to handle all media well if they are to be considered artful performers. The electronic media make it a must. Young managers will have to take the platform to learn this art. Service clubs, hobby groups, fund drives, political gatherings, all such occasions will give young managers an opportunity to practice. They should be required to take such practice as a part of their early experience since it takes time to become good.

The key to the future of our organizations is in our hands. Young managers need the opportunity and the time to practice the skills they will need in top-level jobs if they are to succeed in such jobs. We will need their success.

Practice, practice, practice. Have we given our future president the opportunity to practice his skills for the job today?   [1981]

25   *A New Generation*

It's a shock when your son borrows your tuxedo. But young people do grow up. Not only do they grow up, they often become more able than we ever were—or ever will be. This may be hard to accept, but accept it we must.

Yes, sons and daughters do grow up, and sometimes they become MBAs. If they are impressive as sons and daughters, they are even more impressive as promising young managers. For those of us who learned our lessons on the job, it may not be easy to admit that these school-trained managers are as good as they are. But they are. The present generation of MBAs is an impressive group, and most senior managers who have had any contact with them are the first to admit it.

They are impressive, not only because of their native talents, but also because of the quality of their educational experience. Graduate business curriculums are not as specialized today as they were in the past, and as a result an MBA receives broader preparation in fundamental management processes and in the tools of management. This makes for adaptable and versatile managers who can function effectively in almost any operating environment.

PROBLEM SOLVERS

A recent experience I had illustrates the value of preparation of this kind. At a *Fortune* 500 company I was visiting, I observed a recently hired MBA attacking a marketing problem "scientifically," using mathematical analysis. This young graduate, who, by the way, had not majored in marketing, told me that his problem-solving technique "raised the eyebrows" of a higher-level marketing executive who had had a dozen years experience in the function and who had been a marketing specialist in school. But the young analyst's techniques worked.

The difference in style and approach of this young manager exemplifies the differences between today's MBA and the graduate of the '60s who did things the same way as their supervisors, mainly because they were both products of the same skills-oriented business training. Both the young MBA and his supervisor had had an education that focused strongly on a particular discipline, such as marketing, accounting, or finance. During those years, it was not uncommon for the knowledge a student learned in school to be out of date by the time he or she graduated. Today, however, with the emphasis in business school curriculums on more general problem-solving techniques, graduates are able to cope with the world as they find it.

Knowledge, though, is only one factor in the equation for success. Motivation is another of equal, if not greater, importance, and today's business school graduate has an "advantage" here too. He or she has had to strive harder to secure, hold, and advance in position than young managers of just a few years ago. Difficult economic conditions have played a major role in strengthening and toughening them. In the lush years of the '50s and '60s, however, we had a much weaker force of young managers because they had not had to overcome difficult circumstances or strive to achieve. Things were just too easy for them—to their detriment.

WILLINGNESS TO PAY THE PRICE

The MBAs of the '70s, in contrast, realize that extra effort is the price of success, and most are willing to work longer hours to achieve that success—however they define it. It is interesting, for example, to note the large number of young entrepreneurs—indeed, young millionaires—who are about these days. Obviously, while these young managers may not rise with the sun, they don't set with it either. Contrary to popular opinion, young managers today seem more than willing to work far into the night if they are working on something that has captured their imagination and kindled a spark of enthusiasm.

This new breed of managers has also grown up amid social
turbulence unprecedented in this century . . . and they've witnessed it all on television. These vicarious experiences have given
them an unusually candid and realistic view of life.

Given their heightened sense of realism, you would expect to find
them realistic about the fallibilities and foibles of people too. But
you don't. They still expect their supervisors to be intelligent and
purposeful—and emotionally secure enough to explain the "why"
behind operating procedures and objectives without feeling threatened. The new breed rejects blind obedience to authoritative
management in favor of participatory experience—they want to join
the action, not just follow it. Job participation and satisfaction comes
first with most of them.

Young managers today realize that if they allow themselves to be
diminished on the job, they will be diminished in their personal
lives too. They are interested in a lifestyle that preserves their
dignity, builds their self-esteem, and, at the same time, accords
them a feeling of freedom.

A DESIRE TO CONTRIBUTE

Perhaps this is a main reason why MBAs of the '70s consider it a
privilege to work in the public sector. In the past, such service was
considered the last recourse if a graduate could not find a job in the
private sector, but today about one-third of those currently seeking
an MBA in one school, for example, are headed for not-for-profit
careers. Reason? Their feelings of personal worth and satisfaction
are keyed to what an organization does—what it contributes to
society.

These new MBAs are also critical of government, though, and are
beginning to sense that it is interfering more and more with the
decision-making process of business. "All right," they say, "the only
way to change government is from the inside," so they are applying
for government jobs. They hope to help enact sensible laws and
formulate reasonable regulations, and to ensure that they are
uniformly enforced. Vague laws that leave discretionary powers in
the hands of people who do not understand the decision-making

process and its risks are anathema to them. Undoubtedly, if enough MBAs come to share this attitude, a more intelligent relationship between the public and private sectors will result.

A COMMITMENT TO PERSONAL GROWTH

Having benefited from a broad formal education, young managers will, I believe, concern themselves more with their continuing education than have their predecessors. Managers whose education was more skills-oriented have not as a rule returned to school except to update themselves on new developments in their fields of specialization. I think it will be the mark of managers of the '70s that they will continue to broaden themselves by taking courses both in and outside their special areas.

This broadening will prove most valuable in the decade to come. Both business and government can expect increasing criticism from the public. The young leaders of today will have to respond to this criticism, objectively and intelligently. Their current outstanding performance "under fire" makes me optimistic that they will handle these challenges with sensitivity and grace—and that they will work to improve the general good.

Those who carry the burdens of leadership today can rest easy in the knowledge that a tested cadre of young leaders stands ready to assume the load.   [1977]

PART FOUR

Ethics

26   *Jekyll and Hyde Managers*

Can a manager show one set of standards in private life and another at the office? Spurred by society's broadening acceptance of divergent lifestyles, some thoughtful managers are raising this question. It is a delicate matter, made particularly touchy by our sensitivity to the right of personal privacy—"What I do after five o'clock is none of my company's business"—which has become sacred to many and, at least to some, so potentially litigious.

Setting the Organizational Tone

Cases that spotlight points of possible conflicting interests between self and the organization are not too difficult to find, however. Despite efforts to keep personal and on-the-job activities in separate compartments, private lives are not necessarily so exclusive after all. Like it or not, managers whose lives after five cross, or appear to cross, the lines of basic standards of propriety run certain risks. The trials and tribulations—and transgressions—of private life, for example, often become known to peers, subordinates, and bosses— and not infrequently to the press—as details of common knowledge, if not of common gossip. Whether fact or exaggerations, such reports can easily provoke certain apprehensions both within and outside the organization to the potential detriment of the organization and individuals with a stake in the integrity of their managers and associates.

There is little doubt that most managers deal fairly with subordinates and peers, with customers and suppliers, and with others with a vital interest in how the company conducts its affairs. Even so, some managers and members of the public have expressed doubts about the readiness of top management to probe much below the surface into the full range of ethical issues confronting today's top corporate managements and their managerial hierarchies.

I say "some" managers and members of the public because in any

99

circumstance, some persons believe differently, live differently, and react differently in facing certain life situations and questions involving ethical conduct and related behavior. Generally, it is agreed that the moral and ethical tone in any organization is set at the top—when questions are raised about the corporation, the top team must answer. A few managers, however, tend to harbor suspicions, constantly ready to believe the worst and to ask the nagging questions about how moral the organization really is. Some managers feel we are avoiding certain questions because they either are too hot to handle or, if addressed, would offend someone. It is within this context, then, that questions pertaining to personal versus on-the-job standards are raised, asking in effect: To what extent can we really trust a manager whose moral deficiencies in private obligations—for example, infidelity in marriage or blatant disregard of other commonly accepted family obligations—clash with the basic ethical standards he or she is expected to follow in organizational activities and responsibilities?

CALL FOR ACTIVE LEADERSHIP

The apparent failure—if not unwillingness—of organizational management to research these issues prompts these difficult questions, which in fact may involve not so much the issues of right and wrong as suspicion and doubt. Whatever the root cause, management in general has been put on the defensive and is being challenged by some of the extreme critics to exert a more active brand of moral leadership.

The changing standards and precepts of society have strongly affected the business-personal balance of many managers. While asserting their right to personal privacy, managers more and more live a fishbowl type of existence. Are we then really liberated and free? Or have we, as some critics aver, permitted a deterioration in standards?

CONTRAST WITH THE PAST

The evolution of management's public versus private dilemma provides some interesting contrasts. Industry's early history is marked with examples of how top managers made the moral standards of their employees matters of top concern. Companies and communities were small, and everyone had a public reputation. Character was openly identified, and, for the most part, private lives and business lives were expected to maintain a basic consistency.

Later on, personal reputation and one's job developed a pattern in which what one did was as powerful as what one said. That is, the banker caught stealing lost his job as much because he had violated the integrity of his position in the mind of the public as because he had violated laws against embezzlement. At another level in the hierarchy of personal versus public responsibility, teachers were effective professionals because their community deportment had to be as strong as their professional performance—for example, smoking in public was simply not accepted because it set a bad example for students, who ran great risk of punishment even for experimenting with corn silk.

PRIVATE VERSUS PUBLIC ETHICS

Finally we have reached an era in which business lives and private lives are by common agreement generally kept separate; privacy is a treasured possession, particularly in the big city or in the big company.

But as anyone knows after only a single trip to the water cooler, private lives are not really so private. And regardless of how easily, on the surface at least, society accepts today's one-out-of-two marriage casualty rate, some executives are questioning whether the manager who has been separated or divorced more than once is as reliable as one who has never been divorced. Certainly I don't know, but I do know that many conservative managers are looking for answers. Can a mother or father who "plays the field" or who is indifferent to the welfare of children or a discarded spouse really be constructively sensitive to employees' well-being and maintain an ethically sound managerial posture at the office? There are even those who would also ask a similar question about the working mother who really doesn't need a job but who prefers to take the risks of simultaneously maintaining a home and a job. Some managers wonder whether a person so self-oriented in private matters can be sufficiently self-effacing on the job to cooperate well in a team effort.

No Quick Answer

The quick answer to many of these questions, if put to an individual, might be "It's none of your business." Fair enough. But thousands of managers and workers lose respect for the peer or boss whose private life reveals what they consider glaring weaknesses and inconsistencies in character. They believe, correctly or incorrectly, that consistency in values is important for effective and ethically sound performance on the job. They understand the necessity for a divorce; they are sympathetic to parents whose work requirements necessitate leaving children on their own or in a makeshift home environment. But they worry how the carry-over effect of a moral deficiency in private life will influence the public or organizational moral standards of the manager. Just how much do the ethics of individual managers in their personal affairs influence the standards of organizational ethics?   [1982]

27   *Ethics: To See Ourselves as Others See Us*

Recently I spent a weekend at two different universities in the Midwest. At the first school I met with undergraduates. They were a bit cynical, a bit idealistic, and, while they were acting as if they knew all about the world, curious about what it was really like "out there." At the second school I met with a group of men and women graduates, all of whom had jobs in management. They were curious about *why* the world of management is as it is—in their eyes. These two groups seem to me to reflect the same attitudes and concerns about management that you will find among people in general.

In both meetings there was the usual awkward period in getting a discussion going. After a few polite and obvious questions in each group, a question on ethics came quickly, and this issue dominated the rest of our discussion. And interestingly, the opinions of the two groups were quite similar. But the undergraduates were accusatory while the graduates were serious.

What was particularly interesting was that the graduate group—the managers—also had strong reservations about the ethics of businessmen today, so this meeting was not a case of "preaching to the converted."

A LACK OF MORAL FIBER

When the discussions on ethics started, I was ready for questions on the profits of oil companies, payments to foreign governments to obtain favorable treatment, bribes, economic discrimination, and the other familiar "blockbusters." Surprisingly, both groups were withholding final judgment on these matters. The students seemed to be saying, "I want to believe what managers say about these issues, but they make it so difficult." However, they said in effect that the stance of managers in business on the big issues almost automatically lacks credibility because these same managers have shown a lack of moral fiber when it comes to handling the smaller, everyday ethical issues. The students seemed to define "moral fiber" in this context as a respect for the values of customers and employees and sensitivity to the concerns of society in general.

But the criticism was not of business managers alone, although most of the questions were about them. What the students were saying is that all managed institutions and the people in them are producing a climate of cynicism that discourages those who want to improve things.

At the end of the sessions I asked myself, "What did they learn? Something positive? Or did they despair?" In retrospect it seemed to me that 100 students and almost as many practicing managers took from the meetings a reinforced awareness that people who "fib" are difficult to believe when they tell a great truth and that people barely listen to "fibbers."

The advertising practices of business continue to be a favorite target for criticism. But members of both groups held a wide range of opinions, mostly favorable. The negative comments, however, were generally accepted by group members. For example, current TV advertisements for designer jeans were discussed at length—a brief comedy relief—and these discussions resulted in general condemnation of the apparent lack of sensitivity of advertisers and manufacturers to the moral standards of the general public. One student had clippings that she believed said much about manufacturers' standards and values. For example, a *New York Times* article describing the war of the jeans quoted one manufacturer as saying: "The only ones to survive will be the guys who have imagination, flair, and a lot of money. . . . The jeans companies can be the sportswear houses of the 1980s—with one important addition: television ads." The article continues, "The ads of the Big Four . . . are sexy and daring." Then there were quotes from an article in *The Wall Street Journal* entitled "Some People Believe That Blue Jeans Ads Are a Little Too Blue." Finally, a columnist who said she would be considered "a prude" by many people called these ads indecent, adding that she had forbidden her children to watch TV programs sponsored by jeans companies.

The negative feeling about these ads affected group members' attitudes toward business, advertising agencies, psychologists (some in the groups contended each TV station had one), and the media that would carry such advertising. The discussion revealed much cynicism about how far companies will go under a competitive system to make money. While the logic may not have been unimpeachable, the reaction was both strong and plausible.

REACHING THE "ORDINARY GUY"

Disclosure was another puzzle. How can an "ordinary guy" read an annual report? If these reports and other information aimed at prospective investors aren't reasonably easy to understand, how can the average individual be expected to invest in the stock market? A woman in one of the groups expressed the belief that annual reports were written for institutional investors, financial analysts, big banks, and insurance companies. To her it was symbolic of big business running everything and "shutting out" the little people by account-ing and economic "mumbo jumbo." She really didn't care much about the regulations of the SEC or the interpretations of the FASB. Again, her logic was questionable, but the message was loud and clear: People won't defend what they cannot understand; and institutions do not seem to want understanding from "outsiders."

Newspaper and television journalists did not receive high marks either, although all the participants said they watch television news programs and read newspapers. One of the participants quoted Albert Einstein: "The right to search for truth implies also a duty; one must not conceal any part of what one has recognized to be true." The students expressed the opinion that it is illogical for television to attempt to condense newsworthy items into 30-second reports and expect the public to accept these reports as adequate. And most believe that newspaper headlines and articles are biased toward sensationalism to sell newspapers.

While admitting that there are times when complete candor would be unrealistic, both groups showed little patience with managers—and others—taking defensive positions. They admire managers who "tell it the way it is" and then handle the reactions. "At least they are credible," said one young student. A clear lesson from these reactions is that we in management have a responsibility to test the effects of our behavior on all of those around us.

If managers are careless about basic things—telling the truth, respecting moral codes, proper professional conduct—who can believe them on other issues? Character is indivisible; a flaw is a flaw regardless of the issue. The character of managers is important to those students because they regard managers as particularly influential in our society. They do not mind sharp divisions of opinion or glaring mistakes by managers. But they do object to managers denying or lying about such incidents.

What can we as managers do to deserve, earn, and retain good judgment of our ethical behavior? Something I read recently may offer some help. Robert F. Allen, president of the Human Re-sources Institute, has suggested seven key questions to ask about ethical behavior at work in our organizations: 1. Is ethical behavior being rewarded or penalized by the organization and in what ways?

2. Is this behavior being visibly modeled by leaders within the organization? 3. Are people receiving feedback and information relating to whether they are practicing this behavior? 4. Are the day-to-day interactions and relationships between people supportive of this behavior? 5. Do the organization's formal and informal training programs emphasize this behavior and offer skills in connection with it? 6. How are new people coming into the group being oriented to this behavior? 7. Are time and other resources in the organization allocated in ways that show commitment to this behavior?

If managers want to earn and retain respect, ethics may be a good place to start.   [1980]

28   *Conscience: The Spirit of the Law*

No one ever made money on an expense account, so a little padding brings me out even.

If it takes a few dollars to swing the contract our way, go ahead and use your own judgment.

All this food and drink will be wasted if left here, so we can take it when we leave work.

The board never questions legal compliance unless we are sued, so we will probably never be questioned about this capital expenditure.

Some would say these are musings on unimportant matters. Others might regard them as "winking" at principle. A few would quickly identify laws or regulations that are involved. Aside from these observations, what can be read into every statement is an attempt to get around conscience.

FILTERING OUT GUILT

We don't use the word "conscience" much today because it can produce discomfort, if not guilt. Conscience has been called "the thinking man's filter." If there were no written laws or rules, this filter would still work, telling us that certain things should not be done or, more importantly, that positive action is required of us.

Conscience can be shaped: We can improve its sensitivity or almost destroy it. It reminds me of a person's physique—there is no way to escape having one, but we can do much to shape or destroy it, and we have to work on it every day.

A conscience can become dull with bits of carelessness. Cheating a little bit by being late or leaving early at worst "winks" at a rule. Ignoring a customer because we are tired, or taking out our irritations against the company by doing shoddy work—all these are dullers of conscience. They are so minor that we can easily get away with most of them or rationalize our behavior with deep psychological explanations. But our conscience is a "cur that will let you get past it, but that you cannot keep from barking.'

THE IMPORTANCE OF SMALL MATTERS

A sharp conscience makes little distinction in small issues. It is minor matters that provide it with isometrics. Saying "no," avoiding the "winking," responding to affirmative nudges are the ways we make it strong. It takes much practice to be strong enough to turn down the bribe or refuse the product when there is any question about its safety, purity, or worthiness.

Managers are always searching for this thing called conscience—particularly in others. They talk of "character," "honesty," "integrity," or "trust." But they do not seek these fine qualities in and of themselves. They are looking for something that will permit decentralization and delegation to be attended by sensitive judgment.

This is a worthy demand to make of others, but managers must lead the way and make their own consciences strong. That course in ethics may help. Members of your trade association can assist. And thinking of your religious affiliation is not a bad idea.

One of the ways we avoid personal involvement with our own consciences is to try to depersonalize the issue or situation that confronts us. Today, we hear calls for corporate "conscience," "social responsibility," and "ethical standards." These are directed to legal entities or inanimate structures that have no real conscience. Organizations are made up of people—real human beings—and it is they who possess the consciences. If there were really such a thing as a corporate conscience, then it must be the sum total of everyone in it. No one escapes.

Placing Responsibility

It is too easy to assign responsibility for the corporate conscience to the chairman or president, or to some other senior officer, or just to "management"—although they do, ultimately, hold accountability for the actions of everyone in the organization. When our delivery people are indifferent in their care of the product—because their consciences as individuals are not working—then we apologize to the customers, improve our packaging, and train our delivery people a bit more rigorously. But the person with the lax conscience can still say the wrong thing, arrive at the wrong time, or generally be negative. On the other hand, the clerk who feels that he or she is *the* representative of the company—because of a sensitive conscience—is invaluable in telling the public who and what we are.

The corporate conscience is embodied in the stockholders, the board of directors, the managers, and the employees. It may be students, faculty, and administration. Or it can be voters, elected officials, and government managers. Each person in these groups has a conscience and to some degree becomes part of the organization's conscience—and thus shares in the responsibilities attached to it.

The corporation itself is a legal structure and responds to laws and regulations, but that is a diffferent thing entirely. In the 19th century, Henry David Thoreau, the New England naturalist-philosopher, posed the question: "Did you ever expect a corporation to have a conscience when it has no soul to be damned and no body to be kicked?" Of course, his was a moralistic society where small organizations were easily identified with the owners, and everyone in the community knew who worked with them. Moral training was a part of the liberal education, whether in the university, the church, or the home. Morality was stronger than ethics, and the law was an infrequent recourse for the well-regulated society.

HIDING BEHIND THE LETTER OF THE LAW

Today we work hard at being amoral, or at least legalistic. Managers and those who work with them are sensitive to laws and contracts but often lack the sensitivity of personal responsibility to their own consciences. Novelist Aleksandr Solzhenitsyn spoke forcefully to this issue in his Harvard commencement address last year:

> People in the West have acquired considerable skill in using, interpreting, and manipulating law. . . .Any conflict is solved according to the letter of the law, and this is considered to be the supreme solution. If one is right from a legal point of view, nothing more is required; nobody may mention that one could still not be entirely right, and urge self-restraint, a willingness to renounce such legal rights, sacrifice, and selfless risk: It would sound simply absurd. One almost never sees voluntary self-restraint. Everybody operates at the extreme limit of those legal frames. . . .
> A society which is based on the letter of the law and never reaches any higher is taking very scarce advantage of the high level of human possibilities. The letter of the law is too cold and formal to have a beneficial influence on society. Whenever the tissue of life is woven of legalistic relations, there is an atmosphere of moral mediocrity, paralyzing man's noblest impulses.

Laws may help us a little here and there, but conscience extends to areas that the letter of the law cannot address. The *spirit* of the law cannot be articulated by legalistic phraseology—it is expressed in simple terms and by the "inner voice."

When we are willing to develop that inner voice and heed its counsel, fewer written laws will be needed.   [1979]

29   *The High Cost of Buying Cheap*

"There's no such thing as a free lunch." This expression has been around for a long time. Some managers claim it is an unrealistically cynical attitude. Others, less idealistic, perhaps, accept its essential truth: In the long run, in one way or another, we pay for what we get.

That we get what we pay for and pay for what we get applies in all areas of business. Organizations cannot survive if they do not recover the costs of providing their products or services. And they *will* not stay in business if they do not earn a profit sufficient to make it worthwhile.

The need to recover the costs of providing a service also holds true for not-for-profit and government organizations: If over a reasonable period of time their income doesn't at least equal their expenses, they will cease to exist—or go bankrupt.

WHAT IS "CHEAP"?

What this means, then, is that those who offer a product or a service at significantly less than the going rate must be shaving costs somewhere, in service, quality, credit, guarantees—somewhere. This loss of value and service is the high cost in buying cheap.

How can capital goods be made "cheap"? Well, a manufacturer may be able to pay his employees less than some other manufacturer. And "savings" can perhaps be achieved by taking shortcuts in design. Materials vary in quality and cost, too, so some saving may be achieved there. Also, terms of credit offered may not be so liberal, and service may not be prompt and effective. A product made using all these shortcuts might well be offered "cheap"—that is, for much less than the prevailing price—but would it really be cheap?

How much would maintenance costs be on such a piece of equipment, for example? Cost-conscious manufacturers are buying capital goods using life-cycle costs rather than only initial product cost as the basis for their decision. Life-cycle costing includes not only the initial purchase price but also the costs involved in keeping the equipment in top working order for the full period of its planned use. It considers the cost of downtime attributable to poor service or the lack of readily available parts, and it considers the costs of other manufacturer "savings." An organization buying capital equipment is buying a capability to perform a needed function. If the equipment is out of commission, it is the same as not having it at all. Is that cheap?

Thnk of *your* shopping experiences, too. What is cheap? Is it goods that lack style? Last year's model? Surly sales personnel? Late delivery? No guarantee? Poor service? No credit? A dirty store and damaged goods? Dirty windows and a littered sidewalk? No retailer can provide quality goods, helpful sales people, and other customer-oriented services without recovering the cost of these services. If the retailer doesn't provide them, the customer must— or must do without. Who can afford to buy "cheap"?

PEOPLE COSTS

People provide another example. No organization can buy talented people cheap. When an organization is recruiting its staff, buying cheap will almost always result in buying dear. Educated, talented, motivated people respond directly and indirectly to how their employer treats them. Most people, if they see that their employer respects and values them, will return respect and value; if they perceive an attitude of sharp dealing, they will respond in kind.

People adjust their work behavior to achieve equity—as they see it. If employees think—rightly or wrongly—that they are not being paid at a "fair" level—that is, the going or an honestly negotiated rate—or are not being accorded the respect to which they feel entitled, they will react. They will seek redress, either directly through personal or collective negotiations with their supervisors, or indirectly through malicious obedience, soldiering, errors, tardiness, absenteeism, grievances, and so on. Elliott Jaques, the English social scientist, has demonstrated that people have a concept of felt-fair pay. If they are receiving what they think fair, they respond favorably—and vice versa. This true, can companies really afford to buy "cheap"?

To think only of the near term is also shortsighted. Just as with capital and consumer hard goods, people have a life-cycle cost—and value. When a company employs people, it is buying not only immediate service but also future potential. Future potential springs from the unfolding of all the talents people bring to their work *and* the flexible use of these talents. Just as a plant does not grow in hard and rocky soil, or without water and nurturing, neither do employees unfold in a harsh and constricting environment that shows them little regard for their humanity.

Future potential unfolds when people feel fairly treated and respected for themselves and their talents. When such treatment is lacking, they will leave. Turnover of talented people entails great expense. Not only is the immediate value of their knowledge and experience lost, but training a replacement is time-consuming—and very expensive. Reducing turnover is a money-saving move.

TRAINING AS A MESSAGE

Many companies show their appreciation of and respect for their employees by providing them with training opportunities. These are in addition to the fair pay and benefits and other attractive aspects of employment they receive. When a company offers its employees training, particularly training that will help them realize their full range of talents and make them more valuable to the company, it is telling them not only that it thinks they are important to the company, both today and tomorrow, but also that it thinks they have the potential to continue to grow in their careers. These are highly encouraging messages.

Here again, however, there is a high price for buying cheap.

Training that is professionally prepared and professionally delivered carries the message, "This is an important activity about which we care very much." Casual, unprofessional training delivered on a catch-as-catch-can basis delivers a quite different message. The professional approach to training has both direct and indirect value; the casual approach may have some direct value, but its message is essentially demotivating. What organization can afford to demotivate its employees?

QUALITY BREEDS QUALITY

A quality training experience tells employees that the organization values quality in all that it does. Instilling this attitude in a company's employees should help improve many other aspects of their performance, too, a not insignificant gain.

A quality training experience also ensures that the best possible use is made of the trainee's time, another not insignificant economy.

And when people "travel first class," they see themselves as first-class people, a great boost to their morale—and to their sense of self-worth.

Clearly, then, buying cheap has a high cost. Paying a fair price, however, is buying wisely—and inexpensively.   [1978]

30   *A Right and Wrong?*

Whatever happened to our time-tested concept of a moral code? Has the elusive concept that some people call "value systems," that is, individualized and varying standards of behavior, taken its place?

I know that the old moral codes sounded less flexible. Indeed, that seemed to be their advantage; everyone knew the rules. The concern was not solely with the efficacy of an act but also with its intrinsic "rightness" or "wrongness."

No Two of a Kind

Relativistic morals, on the other hand, are singularly lacking in fixed standards of right and wrong. What is "right" is what fits the situation in which the act occurs. But who is to decide? Your judgment of what fits may not match mine. Consider, for example, the following problem—which, according to the journalist who cited it on a nationally televised morning show, is included in tests given to college students. Here's the gist of it: You stumble upon an open envelope containing a $10 bill and a note bearing a name and address. No one sees you. What should you do?

The journalist contended that there is no single right or wrong answer to the problem. Instead, he claimed, the answer would be relative—depending on the test-taker's *personal* value system. An affluent test-taker who decided to return the money wouldn't be doing the "right" thing, but merely something that was easy and convenient because being honest didn't entail any great personal sacrifice. (A wealthy person doesn't, after all, need the money.) And the test-taker with limited resources who decided to keep the money wouldn't be doing the "wrong" thing because he or she had a greater need for the money than for being honest.

This is nonsense. Keeping the money is stealing, no matter who does it, no matter what the circumstances of the thief. The problem is one that calls for a moral decision against a fixed standard, not a personal value judgment.

What if the amount of money involved were changed—say, to $10,000? Would this mean that even an affluent finder could keep it without compunction because it would be enough to make a difference to him?

A Code for All Seasons

A person's moral code—or lack of one—will affect all phases of his or her life, occupational and social. The employee who lives by a fixed moral code, for example, will take it into consideration when making a business decision. Organizations have the responsibility to nurture moral decisions through the force of the example of their top managers and the managerial behavior they reward. Few seem to be taking this responsibility seriously. Too often in organizations today we hear, "But the end *does* justify the means." To me this is unacceptable.

No end justifies lying, cheating, or stealing. When a number of union members agree to call in sick to force a company to settle a contract difference, that is lying (and conspiracy as well, which compounds the lie). The achievement of their end—the eventual settlement of the contract difference—doesn't make their means right.

It isn't right for an executive to claim that increased profits guarantee more jobs if he is merely theorizing and doesn't have in mind the purpose of producing more jobs. Without the purpose, his theorizing amounts to a lie.

The person who goes on unemployment compensation when work is available to him is stealing. Payroll padding is stealing. The practice of featherbedding is stealing.

Two Disturbing Effects

The national and international news scenes abound with reports of wrong or immoral behavior by people in power. Such revelations about those who have been entrusted with the responsible use of power have had at least two disturbing effects:

- A growing erosion of trust on the part of the American public in the institutions of society.
- A feeling among people that "if the high and mighty can act like that, I can, too—and the sooner I get mine, the better."

Continuing in this direction could leave us with millions of individual "value" systems that would often be working at cross purposes, perhaps with everyone trying to take advantage of everyone else. But more and more I sense that this is not what people want. More and more I sense that people would like to get back to living with clear moral standards. If we would do this, if we would return to broadly shared, fixed moral standards, life might become much more livable for us all.   [1976]

31   *Reputation: The Most Prized Possession*

According to an old fable, a young man told his confessor that he had damaged the reputation of another person in the village. The confessor ordered the man, as part of his penance, to go to the nearest hill and empty a bag of feathers to the wind. After he had done so, scattering the feathers far and wide, the confessor told him to gather up all the feathers again. "Gather them all! Impossible!" cried the young man. "So too with the reputation you have damaged." replied the confessor. "I can give you absolution, but I doubt that you will ever be able to correct what you have done."

Professional managers in the public and private sectors often find themselves involved with other people's reputations. Many of them know things that, if generally revealed, would hurt the reputation of someone on their team, a customer, a vendor, a patient, or a competitor.

These professionals often—even at the risk of taking abuse themselves—make judgments without telling all they know. This is to their credit. I recall the case of a president who happened to discover that his controller had systematically falsified the company's records. He requested the resignation of the controller, who left the company quietly. But when others in the firm learned of his departure, their reaction was anything but quiet. The controller had been well liked and competent, and of course they knew nothing about the record falsification. A vice-president accused the president of being a dictator, and several members of the board criticized him for his "inability to keep good people." Naturally, this was not a pleasant experience for the president, but he silently rode it out so as to preserve the controller's reputation.

This is not as unusual a situation as you might think. Even more common is the "letter of reference" case where a manager is asked to comment on a former employee who has left because he has failed at his job. No manager wants to mislead other managers about a prospective employee. Yet how does he know that one failure will guarantee another? It would be highly presumptuous—and irresponsible—to endanger another person's future on the basis of one's own subjective prediction; discretion here is the better part of valor.

In these cases, at least, the manager has some facts to deal with. He is on shakier ground when falsities and half-facts intrude into the decision process. In both public-sector and private-sector organizations, one hears about "leaks" that crush or threaten reputations. Sometimes such leaks come from disgruntled employees, sometimes from those seeking political advantage in the organization, sometimes from careless gossips, sometimes from malicious busybodies. Since many rumors are only loosely based on truth, managers would do well to check out all negative inputs from "reliable sources." One director of security, told of a guard who had fallen asleep on the job, ordered the guard dismissed—only to learn later, to his dismay, that his tipster had not told him the guard had worked two consecutive shifts because one of his friends was ill.

Organizations have reputations too, and they deserve the same care as do the reputations of individuals. The manager who tries to tarnish the reputation of another organization is recognizing that his own cannot win on its own merits. This does not mean that an organization should never appeal to law, or bring another organization to court, in order to protect its own rights. But stating publicly that another organization *may* be violating the law not only is cowardly and predatory but casts grave doubt on the character of the one who makes the statement. Legal requirements give no one the right to ignore ethical considerations; ethics often begin where the law leaves off.

The credibility of management depends in part on trust. We are (or hope to be) trusted by those who report to us, by those to whom we report, and by those we deal with outside our own organizations. A manager's position of trust requires that he protect the reputations of those with whom he interacts. For, once that trust is damaged, it is as difficult to repair the damage as it would be to put the feathers back in the bag.   [1974]

32   *The Humanity Cycle*

More than a decade ago, many managers were just discovering "human relations," thereby realizing for the first time that there was much more to managing the workforce than just hiring and firing. Since then, there have been a rash of developments in the understanding and classification of human behavior. We now speak of such tools as sensitivity training, and "behavioral science" has become a popular overall term used to describe the full spectrum of human relationships.

We can gain much insight from new developments in behaviorial science. It has contributed greatly to our understanding of how managers may react to given situations and how people generally or statistically react. Such approaches as sensitivity training contribute, too. Sensitivity training helps us to understand ourselves as others see us and adds to our comprehension of why others behave as they do.

HUMAN FACTORS

As our comprehension of human behavior expands, numerous experiments and fads that attempt to improve human relationships are brought to the attention of the public. But regardless of how we change the structural forms of human relationships, we are still working with people who are much the same as before. The human desire for security, recognition, justice, and understanding never disappears permanently.

What many managers fail to understand is that, despite the introduction of more sophisticated means of viewing human behavior, basic human relations will never become outdated. The findings and tools of behavioral science may be more objective than basic human relations, but unfortunately it is possible to have full command of them and still be a boor.

Today's managers have learned from behavioral scientists how to classify people into categories. They declare sensitivity to people and issues thousands of miles away. They know the techniques of implementing programs and procedures dealing with such human matters as job enrichment, manpower development, and motivational communications. But do they know how to deal with the person standing two feet away from them? Are they sensitive to the needs of their own families? Are they aware of the implications for others around them in their current actions?

Good human relations, although it is not a new development, goes far beyond all the more sophisticated and objective approaches to dealing with other people. It returns people from the categories that behavioral scientists have conveniently assembled them into and again recognizes them as individuals.   [1972]

33   *Up from Serfdom*

Drawing on disciplines ranging from mathematics to behavioral sciences, management has become a science in its own right as well as an orderly plan for accomplishment through others. The advancement of management science now affords realistic principles through which a manager can achieve his goals. But the manager who uses these principles must remember that principles alone can lead to dehumanization—just as failure to oil an otherwise effective piece of machinery allows rust to accumulate. Both situations are stepping-stones to breakdown.

Keeping management practices operational through application of large quantities of oil does not require any profound knowledge. The process is so simple that managers often tend to overlook it. It consists of using such terms as "please" and "thank you" when dealing with subordinates. It's the human touch.

It is all too easy for a manager to acquire a sense of superiority to his subordinates and to let this feeling show through in his dealings with them. It would be tragic for management science to have evolved to its present stage if managers are still acting like feudal lords and treating their employees as serfs.

We hope that no form of serfdom exists in our country today. Laws tend to guarantee civil rights to the individual, but usually the best any law can do is to assure minimum civil rights. Politeness recognizes a human right—the dignity of the individual. The importance of human dignity today is well demonstrated in the U.S. Army's current experimental programs that aim at elimination of dehumanizing aspects of military life. The tough sergeant who once growled, "All right, Meathead, get the lead out!" today is learning to say, "Would you please hurry, Private Jones? The rest of the platoon is ready to go."

To veterans of an earlier military era, this change might seem outrageous or, at the very least, humorous. But it's no joke to today's new recruits. Regardless of how menial their responsibilities are, they are equals with whomever they deal and expect to be treated as such.

"Please" and "thank you" are just words, but if they are used properly, they oil the machinery of delegation by telling the subordinate that the manager realizes that he needs help; he cannot do as much alone as he can with others and he recognizes that everyone can contribute to an organized effort, no matter how humble the job or how simple the person.

Similarly, "pardon me" is an acknowledgment of human frailty. It shows the subordinate that we are all alike in our susceptibility to error.

Managers have a broad selection of words that they can use to add the human touch to business relationships. The words themselves are less important than the sincerity of the person using them. Each manager has his own personality and his own way of showing recognition of human dignity or appreciation of work well done; similarly, each subordinate has his own idea of what constitutes dignity and appreciation. If the manager is sincere in his efforts to make the human equation work and equally sincere in his dealings with others, he'll be on the road to success in management's least complicated but most difficult phase—the fine art of human relations. [1971]

34 *Dignity and Social Status*

Although the social order today is more liberal than it was 100 years ago, many people still unconsciously equate dignity with social status. Through this muddled rationale, the manager seems to be afforded automatic dignity by virtue of his status: He has people reporting to him, he makes decisions, and he works with his shirt-sleeves rolled down.

These outer trappings of dignity, though, do not afford dignity in themselves. A manager's real source of dignity is satisfaction that he has done his job well. A decision, then, becomes more than a prerogative of status. It is a responsibility that follows the manager out the office door—to lunch, through recreational activities, and into his family life. Dignity stems from the personal sacrifice made in reaching a proper decision. If this professionalism is coupled with a contribution to society and maintenance of individuality, the manager's dignity is increased even more.

PERSONAL SATISFACTION

Personal satisfaction rarely stems from the manager's job alone. Otherwise, he would have no incentive to leave his office. At home, he might willingly take on the job of repairing a light switch or performing maintenance work on his motor boat, even though he can afford to hire an electrician or mechanic. The manager who gets his hands dirty gains two perspectives: respect for the skilled worker who can bail him out when he attempts work beyond his own sphere of knowledge or experience—and the satisfaction of knowing that he could earn a living in another needed skill if necessary.

A manager's dignity is dependent not only on the ability to move up but also on the ability to move down if necessary and perform a vital function on a lower level. This is what makes the difference between today's manager and members of yesteryear's social caste system. All men today fight to keep jobs, increase security, and maintain dignity. Workers of all kinds have established "bumping" processes so that, if necessary, a job at a lower level becomes available when the need for a higher skill disappears.

INDIVIDUAL DIGNITY

The dignity of the individual is a major issue in today's controversy over welfare practices. Frequently overlooked is the fact that dignity goes with accomplishment and the baseness of human nature with a lack of it. The obvious problems of unemployment stand in strange contrast to the shortage of manpower that surfaces when we speak of cleaning up our cities and beautifying our landscapes. This contradiction has two sides: pluralistic job demands versus a monolithic wage base, and the unrealistic social concern for maintaining the dignity of the individual by restricting his employment to his highest skills.

Human satisfaction and personal dignity know no such restrictions. The "level of work" is a matter of perception. The gifted man has great range, and mowing the lawn is at the lower end of this range, but he still derives satisfaction from it. But the poor man to whom few talents have been given may be returning them all when he does a good job of mowing the lawn. When he finishes, it is *his* job, and it gives him faith in his ability.

Managers can better equip themselves to serve social needs by concerning themselves not only with overviews of such matters as ecology and consumerism, but also with the meaning of work and the problems that have been created for society by artificial restrictions on dignity and the futility of a wage base that builds dependency and a sense of uselessness.   [1971]

PART FIVE

A Social Being

35   *Needed: Activist Managers*

Managers can no longer afford to be like the village barbers of days gone by who were famous for talking every man's politics without revealing their own. The village barber could stand on the sidelines because "government" was a bit remote from his life and business. But today, no citizen can be a spectator because all citizens are affected daily by what their government has done, is doing, and plans to do. And managers are affected more than most.

With the impact of government on our lives so great, it is not surprising that almost everyone complains about the regulatory burden. When 14 cents of every dollar of income goes to buy the services of the one out of five people in the United States who are employed by government, citizens *should* be concerned about what they are buying. Not even the barber—or the hairdresser—is neutral today about government and what it is doing and how. Passive acquiescence to government incursions into what were once private matters is no longer acceptable. Activism is the cry of the day.

JOIN THE FRAY

Public-spirited, responsible activism is a currently popular attitude. But many managers have not yet joined the fray. As leaders in their communities and as intelligent, responsible citizens, however, managers should be in the front ranks. We need more activist managers. How else will managers make known the effect "big" government has on the economy and on job creation? How else will managers convey their concern for the effects of government regulation on the climate of freedom in the country, not only their freedom but the freedom of all citizens? How else can managers make legislators and regulators aware that entrepreneurship, the life blood of free enterprise, cannot survive in a highly regulated economy? And more modestly, but perhaps more importantly, how else can managers convey to these same officials that their assumptions about how organizations are managed are naive?

Managers must share with officers of government their awareness that the bureaucracy and paperwork created by poor laws and extensive regulation dramatically affect consumer prices, suppress the initiative of the citizenry, and perhaps worst of all, foster disdain among the burdened citizens for laws and regulations and for the legislators and government employees who create or enforce them.

No Wishful Thinking

The judgment that managers have much to contribute to better government should not be taken to suggest that *all* managers deserve emulation. No whitewash here. Amateur managers do succumb to greed and dishonesty at times. So do doctors and lawyers and engineers and workers—no more, no less. To protect the community from the deviant few, however, government should introduce only essential regulation. The issue is how much.

Although business people may well think that regulation has gone too far, it is wishful to think the clock can be turned back. Practical wisdom suggests that we not look back to undo what already is but that we rather look forward—no matter how small the opportunity—to prevent or at least shape the laws and regulations that will be upcoming as time goes on. Let's build a dam against the flood rather than work to drain the swamp.

Fortunately, legislators and appointed government officials are receptive in most cases to widespread, public-spirited reactions of the business community. Most officials, being committed to doing the best job they can, and to being fair, seek expert advice, but too often the response of managers belies the sincerity of their cry that "something must be done." When given the chance, too many managers do nothing. Even if they feel the need to be active, even proactive, they hesitate to stand as individuals to be heard. They are much more comfortable working anonymously through the collective voice of a trade association or other group. Such groups are good, but their sounds are muted in contrast with the sharp, clear voice of a well-informed and highly concerned individual.

Let's change. Let's become dedicated citizens and spokespeople for what we believe. And if we believe that the free enterprise system and professional management have much to offer to our country and to people everywhere, let's spend time and talent helping to persuade legislators and officials of the validity of our views.

Two Opportunities

Two modest opportunities exist right now for management activists to help shape important legislation and regulations. These are new, emerging issues on which political opinion has not formed as I write this. Management opinion has, though, and that gives us a basis for action.

The first opportunity involves the paperwork burden federal regulation has placed on business. Several months ago the federal government created the Federal Paperwork Commission. The commission completed its work and dissolved on January 31, 1978. It had a short but very effective life—a good sign in itself. Before its demise, the commission proposed that an executive order be issued requiring that before a regulation becomes law, those affected by it must be heard. More than this, though, the proposed order requires that all federal agencies establish regular cycles for the review of all their existing regulations. Here, then, is a great opportunity for the business community, for the management activist.

Think of the significance of this one small proposal. The possibilities for influencing the shape and character of regulation to ensure its sensibility are so great that every organization should structure and staff itself for a systematic response. One approach might be to have the corporate secretary track regulations and reviews and alert managers who would be affected by regulatory changes. Perhaps some other approach would work better, but it seems clear that leaving the monitoring to each manager would be the worst way to go.

The second opportunity is in the proposed changes in the structure and functioning of the federal Civil Service system. The President has proposed the first major overhaul of the system since its creation in 1883. How his proposal will fare in Congress is anybody's guess, but those parts of it that call for the use of sound management practices are worthy of every professional manager's support. The changes he proposes will provide for more flexible hiring and promotion practices and for practices that will rely less on paper examinations than at present; they stress the use of performance standards and the evaluation of people against these standards; and they provide improved procedures for separating poor performers and rewarding good ones. Keeping in mind the potential for abuses in handling personnel in political institutions, the proposal also provides expeditious appeal channels for employees to protect them against arbitrary decisions. And the proposal assigns more responsibility to government managers to make the day-to-day personnel decisions. With this restructuring of accountability, the focus will be on good management.

Managers and business people in general can no longer afford to wring their hands and wail in dismay about the encroachments of big government on their domain while they do nothing to affect legislation and regulatory efforts. They must become activists. Paperwork and civil service reform are two issues worthy of their talents.   [1978]

36   *Political Neuters*

Many of today's managers can still remember one of their parents advising them, "If you want to get along with other people, there are two subjects that you should never discuss—religion and politics." The case for being cautious about initiating religious discussions may still hold true today, for the effect of attacking another's deeply held beliefs is rarely constructive.

But in a free society, where it is not only the right but the responsibility of citizens to exercise their franchise to select their government, any attempt to stifle open discussion is injurious to democracy. Managers, because of their influential and sometimes exposed positions, sometimes feel that they must maintain an external air of political neutrality. They fear that expression of their views might jeopardize their positions within the company or hurt the company with its customers, or that it might inhibit subordinates who do not agree with them.

TAKING A STAND

If managers were to shy away from political involvement, though, this would be depriving society of the views of its most effective leaders and opinion shapers. Politics is at its worst when leaders can be muzzled—and so is democracy. Perhaps a barber can be told that he can take any side on any issue as long as his customers return, but this is hardly a worthy posture for a manager. The man of courage can take a position and still make a customer, superior, or subordinate feel comfortable in holding another position.

In expressing his views, the manager has two additional responsibilities: He must make it clear that his views are his own, not his company's, and he must be careful not to intimidate others whom he has influence over. Even so, there may be attempts to associate his views with his company by those who are too quick to read between the lines. In such instances, it is the responsibility of the manager to stand firm and that of his associates and superiors to stand by his right to act as an individual member of society.

Many companies have taken positive steps to encourage employees to take an active interest in political campaigns and have, at the same time, avoided the appearance of directing their personal lives. One example of this is a program at Hughes Aircraft run by a temporary organization with a nonpartisan section—registration and contributions—and a partisan section—political rallies and information.

Two vice-presidents, one for each major party, serve as the partisan section's chairmen throughout the company, and there are two similarly aligned political coordinators in each plant who are chairmen of their parties' local volunteer booster committees. In four election years, beginning in 1964, 17,000 employees have been registered as voters in-plant, more than 300 candidates have appeared at plant-site rallies, more than $421,000 has been donated to candidates and parties by nearly 30,000 employees, and 95 percent of those eligible turn out to vote on election day.

In this company and in those with similar programs, managers who have the courage to express their convictions earn the respect of their fellow workers. They challenge others to carefully consider their responsibilities to their country, and—acting with the sense of responsibility and taste of a good manager—they ensure that others also have the opportunity to express their views freely.   [1972]

37   *The CEO's Hair*

There's an old saw that says, "You can't delegate a haircut." But in the mid-70s the presidents of many for-profit and not-for-profit organizations may be missing the wisdom of this truism. In these eventful days many chief executive officers may be underplaying their role because of a lack of interest in certain of their long-standing responsibilities or a lack of sensitivity to new responsibilities of great social impact.

SOCIAL JUSTICE

No president, for example, can delegate responsibility for achieving social justice in his or her own organization. Defining what is social justice and striving to achieve it are—and always have been—primary responsibilities of a CEO. It is unfortunate that legislated requirements for affirmative action to redress past social injustices, for example, have seemed to *force* this concern on to top management. But it is much more regrettable that some CEOs have not given affirmative action the attention it needs. Affirmative action programs will work only if they are integrated with organizational efforts for manpower development and career planning, and measured and controlled through the use of turnover statistics and of the promotion rates of affected groups. Personnel and training people, even those committed to equal opportunity, need the forceful leadership and clear policy guidance of top management on this issue if they are to be effective in overcoming past wrongs.

No CEO can delegate responsibility for the effects of his or her own organization's operations on the physical environment. Without question, it is irritating to be accused of malice when your operations cause unexpected environmental harm or to have to adjust your procedures with every change in the wishes of society— but that is the real world. Informing the various groups in the community of the tradeoffs that may be involved in meeting their often-conflicting expectations demands a sure hand at the top of the organization. Giving the community the facts, avoiding threats, being flexible—these require the "big" man or woman, usually the CEO.

ETHICAL POSTURE

No president can delegate the responsibility for setting the ethical posture of his or her organization. The tone of the organization with regard to such matters as its compliance with the spirit as well as the letter of the law and its moral dependability emanate from the top. The right, indeed, the necessity, to fight for its convictions should be part of an organization's moral tone. But in the United States today, a silent fear of retaliation seems endemic. Speaking up about government's distorting intervention in the economic life of the country brings the threat of retaliation—against those who speak out and against the group as a whole. Open discussion of the faults of one power group in the community brings sharp verbal retaliation from members of this group who remember the faults of other groups, such as unions, a minority, or just "some law." Nevertheless, a reasonable defiance of unwarranted and ineffective intervention of any group in the economic or social life of the country may be the sign of strength others need to encourage them to express similar thoughts—and to oppose by action, lawfully.

MANAGEMENT SUCCESSION

No president can delegate responsibility for planning the broad pattern of management succession in his or her organization. Continuity of an organization is not just a matter of its financial stability but also of knowing that the organization will have the leaders it needs in the future. The mechanics of planning a program of succession can come from an organization's manpower specialist, but recognition of the need for such a program and the drive for its implementation must come from the top. Still, it takes a secure CEO to push the growth of individuals who have demonstrated that they have the ability to cope with a future for which even he or she may feel inadequately prepared. No one else in an organization, however, can provide that push.

No chief executive officer can delegate responsibility for control. "Controls," yes, but not control. The financial officer or controller can and should master the controls needed for effective operating management, but the kind of control that determines where an organization fits into society, what its future will be, and what will happen to its people—that's the CEO's hair.   [1976]

38   *The Right Place to Be*

There is a social disease known as "the right place to be." If managers really want to communicate with the people who will ultimately decide how business will be run, "the right place to be" may be the wrong place to be: Sending missions to the cathedral does not convert many pagans. Nor will missionaries talking to missionaries do much more than reinforce the missionary spirit.

Recently I attended a meeting of top authorities in communications. In the course of the discussions, some very unfair generalities about big business were expressed. Managers of big businesses, for example, were accused of insensibility, isolationism, and selfishness. Most of those in attendance at the meeting were men and women from small businesses, professionals from middle management, and a few academicians. Since many of the accusations made were so patently wrong, and no one else seemed to be ready with a defense, I tried, rather unsuccessfully, to put the record straight. But where, I asked, were those best qualified to defend big business—the leaders of large companies?

The experience aroused my curiosity, so I inquired as to the kinds of people who had been invited. "All the corporate leaders in this city" was the answer. Why had none of them accepted? Several of them *had* called about the meeting program, I was told, and to inquire "Who has accepted so far?" The motivation for the question seems clear: They wanted to know if other executives like themselves would be attending.

We all like our cliques, meetings with friends, and invitations to join an "exclusive" group. Such social occasions massage our egos and make life a bit more tolerable. But they do not help much in gaining an understanding of other people's points of view—or in acquainting them with ours. Usually "believers" are in the same crowd; little is gained by complaining to each other that "no one really understands us."

ONE HONEST PERSON

It takes a pile of propaganda to substitute for one honest person. No organization that wishes to be understood can make much headway without the personal involvement of its leaders. Much can be done by articles and brochures and TV and advertising. But none of these can substitute for a person, someone who is physically present and reacting spontaneously to the questions and discussions. You can't question or challenge a radio, TV, or newspaper presentation. The sincerity with which an opinion is offered can come through such impersonal media presentations, but not as well as in a face-to-face meeting. After all, good public relations are based on "good" facts and good attitudes—expressed in actions by good people. A written lie does not make truth; a good deed does.

THE "RIGHT PLACES"

American businesss executives *must* go to the truly "right places." They should be in meetings such as the one I described. They should be in third-world countries. They should be in colleges and universities. They should be in government offices and hearing rooms. They should be in our ghettos. For business leaders to be constantly talking only to each other would seem to me to be irresponsible indifference to an important duty; namely, to represent their organizations' interests with significant nonbusiness groups. Would a salesperson selling a product, for example, spend all his or her time talking to other salespeople?

Those outside of business management, who do not know how managers think, feel, decide, sincerely want to know. They have no interest in passive listening or symbolic agreement, though. They want to discuss and perhaps argue business-related issues that are important to them—but they want to do it with the leaders of businesses, those who can effect changes. Some small-business leaders are staunch defenders of business and management, but many nonbusiness groups feel that the absence of the heads of large businesses is evidence that "we aren't good enough for them to be here—meeting with us isn't the right place to be." The result? Unspoken antagonism where support could be helpful.

GO TO THE ACTION

Business leaders are not alone in their reluctance to meet their publics. I recall one government official who canceled a talk when he found only 100 people would be present. The 100 will never forget this. A local superintendent of schools failed; his successor was very effective. The difference? The new superintendent showed up where the action was—at bazaars, picnics, and meetings—places most of us avoid—and was welcomed. The value of "pressing the flesh" is something every politician knows.

So while politicians can learn much from business about management, managers should be humble enough to admit that they can learn something from politicians. Some lessons are long overdue. Once learned, though, I think we will find many more managers in the truly right places. [1977]

39   *Corporate Governance*

Legislation, administrative rulings, and court decisions have in the last few years emphasized the responsibilities—and increased the potential liabilities—of boards of directors. If you sit on a board, you will sense a heightened interest among the members in the performance of the organization and a greater concern over relationships with its many "publics."

Historically, boards of directors or trustees have ranged in character from being mere figureheads to being the real managers of the operation. But change is touching them all: Attendance at meetings has improved and searching questions are being asked. People invited to stand for election to boards are asking questions, too—and many decline the honor after asking themselves, "Do I have time to become actively involved in this organization? Will I be able to get enough information about its operation, its problems?"

NEEDED: A ROLE DEFINITION

A major question asked by board members and presidents alike is, "Where exactly does the board fit in with corporate life and decision making?" Surprisingly, few boards have formally defined their roles. To be sure, I have never known a board that, collectively, didn't know its legal responsibilities, wasn't keenly conscious of the share-holders' investment, or wasn't concerned about employee welfare. But there has been—and is—confusion over the board's relationship to the organization's management.

Much of this confusion relates to the composition of the board. One made up of "insiders," for example, is frequently a confused board. How can insiders effectively control their own actions? All too often in such cases, the end result is mutual back-scratching. Yet control is an obvious board function.

THE "AGREEABLE" BOARD

Even a board composed mostly of "outsiders" may find it difficult to disagree with management. Members of such an "agreeable" board are usually anxious to adjourn—after receiving their envelopes. But how can *any* board presume that managers—who, after all, are human beings, too—have no need for approval, encouragement, and constructive criticism? The best that can be said of such a board is that it meets regularly. But if its prudence ever comes into question, a record of regular meetings won't go far in its defense. Both these boards and "inside" boards could be helped by professional directors.

At the other end of the spectrum, a "dominant" board often wastes time on second-guessing managerial operations. At one board meeting I attended, the president acknowledged a minor error in judgment—only to have the board waste hours discussing why the error occurred. The efficient allocation of board time is just as important as the efficient allocation of executive time. A clear definition of the board's function can help the chairman get it to "stick to business."

The way board succession is handled can complicate or alleviate some of these problems. Board members are typically replaced one or a few at a time, often by people who serve on other boards. The presumption that service on other boards equips a person to function effectively on a new board often results in cursory orientation—perhaps over lunch by the chairman or president. But as pressures from increased exposure to liability suits grow, every board member should insist on an adequate orientation, one in which questions can be asked and answered. Anything less than a full day's orientation for an experienced director is of questionable value.

USING THE BOARD

While not all experts agree on every aspect of a board's role, most believe that the chief executive officer who avoids using directors as overseers of management performance is acting unwisely, if not imprudently. Presidents and other top-echelon managers may use the board as a voice of conscience, a control mechanism, a sounding board, or an endorsing agent—but they *should* use it.

Of course, it isn't always comfortable to have trusted friends disagree with us. And it is unpleasant when they reprimand us or inquire about and perhaps reverse a decision. But it is precisely this kind of check that keeps us on the right track. As professional managers, we owe it to ourselves to encourage this kind of active board participation. [1976]

40   *Family and the Corporation*

If you looked down on the roof of the Pittsburgh Pirates' dugout during the world series, you saw in huge letters: THE FAMILY. The team's 38-year-old patriarch, Willie Stargell, described it something like this:

> We're a family. We help each other to win. All of us belong to the family—our wives, our children. When anyone makes a mistake, we all help him get over it and forget it, because we are all going to make one sooner or later. But we have to win now—this game.

While some may speculate about the aptness of the Pirates' description of a sports organization as a family, those who know them well detect a real sense of community. Managers in business and industry have been trying to build a sense of community, or at least contribute to it, for years. Many have settled for something called "social responsibility," but that concept is so broad it has almost become a "buzz phrase," embracing a series of activities that help a community, a group, or a cause. I feel uneasy about it because it falls short of the unifying spirit that makes—or puts spirit into—a community. It is more like a contribution or a gift and misses any sense of cohesive force.

THE WHOLE VERSUS THE PARTS

Justice demands that we help disadvantaged groups. Fostering the arts, volunteering for public service, aiding hospitals and universities—who could quarrel with these concerns? But in focusing attention on the problems of these groups, we tend to miss opportunities to promote the power each has to help the others and thus build a fundamental unit of society that I call community.

Building community is becoming more and more difficult as various groups, pursuing their own legitimate interests, tend to stratify society. In working to solve its own problems, each group usually assumes that if each gains what it wants, a good community automatically results. This has many of the same subtle fallacies as believing that if each stratum of an organization achieves an ideal situation, the whole organization will be healthy. When workers attain their union goals, professional middle managers are satisfied, and top management is fairly compensated, has the organization achieved nirvana? It may be closer to bankruptcy.

Most experiments in group motivation bring various strata together in task-oriented formations that share the organizational purpose, not what we might term "strata purposes." Failure to identify the vertical dependencies while stressing horizontal concerns causes problems in many otherwise well-focused projects. European efforts to establish codetermination—worker participation in management—encounter difficulties for this reason. Similarly, that investors gain a return, minorities their shares, government workers security, and business its profits does not necessarily add up to a healthy community. Community builds on giving to all groups, not getting from all.

SELF-GENERATED COMMUNITY

A town or neighborhood generally does better at producing its own discipline than depending on or reacting to outside force. In Pittsburgh, the Mellons got their return and the Democratic administration of Mayor David Lawrence got security when the rejuvenation of a once smoke-marred industrial metropolis became more important than either faction's isolated gain in the early 1950s—and everyone won in the region now dominated by the famed Golden Triangle. Kansas City's Crown Center and the Minnesota Project of Minneapolis are other examples of community dedication. In small towns, merchants clean the sidewalks, and doctors often contribute their talents to the village clinic. In Saranac Lake, N.Y., workers decorate the floats for the ice carnival. This is quite different from contributing money to a cause in a vague wish to fulfill social responsibility.

Less than 50 years ago the push for national ownership of stock began. It made sense to raise capital for growing enterprises by appealing to investors beyond the company's home-plant neighborhood. In the beginning the drive separated big business from small business, and only a few anticipated the evils of absentee ownership. When the proxy placed power in the hands of management, corporate directors generally tried hard to use it wisely, but in the end community gave way to return on equity. Many firms subordinated their local identities to what they regarded as a more rewarding national prominence.

Corporate growth obviously has been good for the national economy; the general pattern is valid. But some casualties have occurred, not the least of which is loss of community. Absentee ownership and concentration of power spawn many kinds of suspicion, creating "haves" and "have nots" in communities that have little to do with the corporation but play host. Banks often have the same experience when they start branching.

SEARCH FOR NEW ROOTS

Big cities suffer along with the smaller ones. The big organizations in metropolitan headquarters too often have had little opportunity for community—the company, as others often see it, belongs to "those out there." Thus the city frequently belongs to no one, except perhaps the graffiti artist and the thoughtless who litter streets, double park, and don't care who runs for office.

Corporations—and unions—are beginning to search for answers; many have done the right things. Some have moved annual meetings to cities having concentrations of stockholders. Ma Bell sends top managers out to visit shareholders in their homes. Others have established ombudsmen, and "better communication" has become the order of the day. We see officers at fund-raising dinners night after night, and corporate generosity supports every type of social effort. As a group, the business establishment is doing more than others. But the vital link between business and the community is difficult to forge; much work remains.

MANAGING THE COMMUNITY EFFORT

There is little doubt where responsibility lies, and corporations— the steel industry, oil producers, chemical manufacturers, utilities, to name some of the most active—are making major efforts to lead thinking on crucial issues. But most of these campaigns are aimed at a national, sometimes a worldwide, audience. Vital local concerns are too often subordinated to the broader issues.

Why can't managements concentrate more effort in a neighborhood approach—say, the development of a community annual report that explains how the company is approaching local problems and benefiting local communities? Present reports are institutionally oriented by regulation and, though stunning in format and crammed with facts, they don't quite mesh with the need for effective community-level recognition and contact.

What we call social responsibility needs deeper thought, if it is to really matter. Those in the executive suite have a major role to play, and they need help from educators, government, and others in finding ways to work creatively for neighborhood identification, not just faceless equality and political strata.

"Social responsibility" makes good talk and reading. But it must spring from a motivation for giving that goes deeper than sweeping concerns about the entire social structure. It needs more than money—specifically people and their time, management and its skills focusing on community at the local level. And this means going beyond even the champion Pittsburgh Pirates and their baseball "family."   [1979]

41   *A Manager's Social Dilemma*

Social responsibility is a current corporate pressure that poses an interesting dilemma for the manager. Does he respond to the pressures of society by making more jobs available for the disadvantaged, while possibly sacrificing job standards, or does he respond dramatically to one form of "consumerism" by culling out poor workers to improve quality?

This situation is complicated by the manager's dual role of businessman and citizen. Eight hours of decision making may not be as irritating as sixteen hours of citizenship outside the office. Both roles are "society in action."

PESKY PROBLEM

Some managers treat social pressures as another pesky problem that is normal to making a profit, like labor troubles, the ringing telephone, or endless meetings. Fortunately, most managers know that it is far more serious. Not only are underprivileged lives involved directly, but the free lives of all citizens will be affected by management's solution to the dilemma of social responsibility.

The mechanistic solutions have been fairly well implemented by managers. More jobs have been extended to minorities. Managers have given thousands of hours of service to national, state, and community organizations to search for answers to problems of housing, schooling, poverty, and work opportunity. Their efforts have created for minorities more income, pride, and eventually, recognition based on merit. But it takes time—long, long years.

Although time allows a generation of underprivileged people to "catch up," probably the most important attitude in changing the social environment has been overlooked by the most progressive and liberal managers as well as by crusading citizens whose chief activity appears to be criticism of the business community and its products. This attitude is patience. If jobs are to be provided and if the privilege of honest employment is the first step leading to a man's rightful place in society, then bringing untrained people into the workforce will result in inefficiencies that will carry penalties, both for management and for consumers. Without patience, society aggravates the dilemma that it asks managers to quickly solve.

PRICE OF PATIENCE

Recently, while I was placing a telephone call to Montreal, the operator asked me: "What state is that in?" If my telephone call is not handled correctly, if petty thievery annoys me, if a mailroom clerk or worker does not respond with insights to my problems, is it not possible that patience is the price I must pay while those with less educational opportunity and a lack of job experience come to a level of competence that allows the forces of efficiency and quality to operate?

There is a Mrs. Van de Van somewhere who is all too ready to criticize the local telephone company when she cannot reach the chairman of her "Committee on Economic Justice." Or, there's Charlie Crusader, who will attend the annual meeting of Consolidated Automobile Company and cast his handful of proxies for two issues: provide more jobs for the socially deprived, and upgrade the quality of CAC's product by providing better workmanship. Meanwhile CAC's managers wonder how to resolve Charlie's issues without suffering a drop in earnings.

Sensitivity to social responsibility should force many managers to look to their training and development efforts. Learning how to train people faster and thereby shorten negative experience is one way to handle social issues. Only the most progressive, analytic, and scientific approach to training and development will do this. The use of every worthy outside opportunity for rapid inputs is important. Pedantic, long-range efforts will subject management to much abuse by well-meaning but shallow thinkers and will invite government stop-gap measures that only delay the solution of good training. The dilemma of social responsibility can best be solved through education.   [1970]

42   *Is Society Our Enemy?*

Today's headlines would have one believe that corporate management is an element outside of society that must be controlled by laws and public pressure lest it continue to go along its merry way— polluting the environment, promoting the supremacy of the WASP, and bilking the consumer. Management's reaction to such criticism often seems to be one of defensiveness. For example, most corporate annual reports now include sections stating that the company is cognizant of today's social ills and how it is taking action to correct them; many companies have invested in major programs primarily designed to combat public criticism.

It may be that management has spent so much time responding to criticism that managers are beginning to believe that they are truly outside of society. It is true that each manager has a responsibility to society, but it is easy to forget that each member of society also has a responsibility to him. How often does one ever hear corporate management, speaking as a segment of society, ask for help from other segments of society—government, religion, and educational institutions?

Management does have a responsibility to society, and it cannot transfer its responsibility to other segments of society—but neither can it do an effective job of accepting simple formulas that are predestined to failure. How many companies, for example, have thrown all principles of sound management out the window in their attempts to placate the public by instantly providing jobs for underprivileged minorities? Even with the best of intentions, the manager who fails to use the tools he has acquired—such as job descriptions and standards of performance—when he is working for society ultimately does a disservice to society.

When working for the public good, a manager cannot stop being a manager. The principles of management contain the basic elements of self-regulation and provide a logical means by which objectives may be achieved. If public pressure appears to contraindicate professional management, the manager must then be as willing to question the standards of other segments of society as they were to question his.

The professional manager asks: Is government providing a climate that allows industry to work toward public betterment without jeopardizing its own health and ultimately that of the public? Has organized religion set a moral or ethical base for norms in conduct that are conducive to good human relations? Have educational institutions done their best to dispel ignorance and to develop young minds to think and make judgments after considering both sides of an issue?

Other institutions cannot escape their responsibilities to society. They must set standards for improvement, provide conditions allowing for it, and condition minds to work toward it judiciously. Then it is management's job to implement improvement. So when a manager feels outside of society, he is wrong. He has the responsibility of interpreting good intentions and generous community gestures into action by seeing that members of his team have the tools and motivation to get the job done.

After the manager has ensured that his own house is in order, he can take some strong stands of his own—and indeed should—that the church, education, government, and other segments of society fulfill their obligation to him by giving him individuals of sharp conscience, good judgment, ability to think, and honest concern for his economic realities so that he can do his part to make his segment of society responsive. [1971]

43   *The Shape of the Product*

Almost daily, we read references in the business press to the effect that the American economy is becoming increasingly service oriented and less production oriented. We agree to this; we see proof of it all around us. Then we make our business decisions on the basis of a manufacturing-oriented economy. We speak in terms of "productivity"—one of the key buzz-words of the year, a manufacturing term—then we coldly calculate how we can produce the product more cheaply, pour more money into advertising, and await the results.

And with all of our astute mathematical planning, sometimes the results aren't as planned. And sometimes we even become "victims" of consumerism, despite the fact that we produce a good product. Why is it that we continue to speak only in terms of products when even consumer groups have become more sophisticated than this?

For example, a group was formed three years ago and recognized by Mrs. Virginia Knauer, Special Assistant to the President for Consumer Affairs. This group, the Neighborhood Consumer Information Center, was formed, according to its executive director, Joe Smith, to "help my people effectively use the power that their earnings and their rights give them to achieve *benefits and services* to which they are rightfully entitled." Mr. Smith didn't say products, did he? He said *benefits and services*.

Benefits and services may include a product or they may be in themselves an item of exchange that cannot be held in one's hand. Classical economics describes the simple fact of exchange as being a transfer where both parties feel they are getting a greater value than the one they are giving up. If I buy a table for $100, I obviously get more satisfaction out of having the table than the $100, and the merchant gets more satisfaction out of having the $100 than the table. But this is only true at the moment of exchange and shortly thereafter.

Suppose now that the merchant no longer carries stock but must order from the factory. Suppose the table is to be delivered Thursday. The merchant may end up with the $100 or a deposit and I postpone my satisfaction until the promised Thursday. But if the table is not delivered then, the satisfaction curve goes down, and if grumpy clerks fail to explain the delay, the downward slope of the curve is accelerated. In time, I reach the point at which I'd rather have my $100 than have the table. When delivery is finally made, there is no company whose table will withstand my inspection. My satisfaction curve is at zero. Now I will join a consumer movement, question the earnings of the corporation that made the table, and in general transfer my hostility to all corporations. If the table company cannot solve this problem, others in the business world who are trying harder to solve this problem would be better off if that company "went under."

Where does hostility show up on the bottom line? It doesn't. It shows up on the top line—sales. Accountants are very good at showing how you can produce more with fewer people, less overhead, and less capital equipment expenditure. But all cost cutting is merely an exercise if you have nothing that the consumer wants—or if you have something the consumer wants, but not enough to tolerate your organization for.

Goods and the time required to produce them are measurable, and the ability to use mathematics properly to do his job well makes the accountant a happy man. Managers, by necessity, are a less happy lot. They have to measure the balance sheet against what they see and know—that unpredictable area of sales. That unpredictable area includes all those things that look bad when you measure overall "productivity." How much corporate productivity comes from such areas as credit and collections, delivery, customer services, or employee relations? And how much business is lost because production and sales personnel are given objectives and

these people aren't? Or because these departments are forgotten
when it's time to put the figures down on paper?   [1972]

44   *Standing on Both Feet*

"Managing our type of organization is different." This great universal statement was repeated the other day as I was meeting with a
group of small businessmen. "Obviously the big company needs
professional management," said the leader of the group, "but our
little companies are different. We need some capital and some
advice, and then our people can make it." This led to a discussion of
new small businesses and the number of these that are off to a wrong
start, particularly those serving minority interests.

Just about any business can use capital and advice, but neither
may be the key to success. There is reason to believe that some
loans to small business are utterly devoid of any serious attempt at
creating a lasting organization. There is further reason to believe
that some types of advice are designed to create dependency rather
than freedom. A serious attempt to help minority enterprises to be
successful should start with our best efforts to have them managed
by professional managers.

The myth still persists that managers are born that way. They
have a special charisma or mystique. They are intuitive. All these
words add up to the fact that some people have it and some have it
not. Once you reason this way, it is easy to move to the dogma that
certain races, one sex, or some particular ethnic background yields
managers more readily than others. Both types of reasoning are
false.

Since the turn of the century enough has been learned about
managers that much of this can be organized and taught to others. If
the learner is then placed in a good decision-making environment,
his chances of success are considerably enhanced.

Many of our minority enterpreneurs are being deprived of the chance of survival because little attention is being given to making them managers at the same time that they obtain a loan. The best money any loan agency could spend would be in developing the manager himself before granting the loan. The question is not whether the loan can be repaid but rather whether the minority enterpreneur will be successful on his own many years from now. This means he must have done his planning very thoroughly before looking to a loan. Does he know how to surrender his personal skill in order to organize the efforts of others?

Instead of this aid in making for success, he often is loaded with such skills as bookkeeping, advertising, and bidding on contracts. These are fine but are not the keys to long-term success. Unfortunately, many minority enterprises have failed with highly accurate records as to why.

Nor is an endless influx of consultants the answer. When starting up or when a problem occurs, then the reputable consultant is needed, but one who wants to manage for another on a continuous basis is probably a quack. The manager may not know how to keep the books, handle the advertising, or get the loan, but he always knows what the books say. He can tell whether the business is improving, and eventually he is free to go to the bank himself. The minority entrepreneur wants to stand on his own feet.

Professional management generally has social responsibility for the success of these new managers. They may be competitors some day. More likely they will be fellow managers in successful organizations. Professional managers should help these new managers get good starts to make increasing loan levels pay off in success and help these managers stand on their own feet as early as possible. [1972]

45   *Consumerism: Stage III*

In today's buyer-seller environment, the term *caveat emptor* constitutes fighting words. Few sellers can speak of "letting the buyer
beware" without being labeled as unethical or worse. But what is
true in this stage of the business world was not entirely true a
century ago.

Caveat emptor, if a selfish philosophy, was at least reasonably
appropriate in an era when the consumer was concerned with
simple matters such as buying a wheel for a cart or selecting fresh
produce from a roadside stand. When we buy fresh produce today,
we still enjoy the responsibility of picking out the ripest, freshest
fruits and vegetables. And the man who bought a wheel for a cart
years ago knew exactly what to look for, because a few years earlier
he had built his own cart, including the wheels.

But then we entered the stage of specialization. People were
buying automobiles, and few of them knew enough about their
construction and capabilities to challenge the authority of the seller.
More and more food was being bought in cans, bottles, boxes, and
frozen packages; the consumer had to rely on what the label told
him—and often packaging standards were so loose that it was
impossible to compare relative quality and quantity of two different
brands.

The confusion created by the technological revolution brought
the marketplace into its second and present stage: one where the
government has taken on the role of protecting the consumer from
his lack of knowledge. This implies that government is more
responsive to society than is business, education, or health services.

Although much legislation is well intentioned, there will always
be some silly laws and some incompetents administering them.
There are even agencies that will push for the practice of poor

management as the norm for "compliance" with the law. Although these are merely exceptions, business is perhaps better qualified than government to protect the consumer. Certainly merchants get "told off" as often in a day as any government official—and they are closer to the problems that need correcting.

Also, the government tends to be confusingly legalistic. Sometimes the assistance it gives the consumer compares with the road signs that a driver must watch while driving 50 miles an hour: He can't find the sign directing him to East Snowshoe because it is obscured by other signs indicating hours of parking, emergency conditions, and directions to destinations hundreds of miles beyond it. Is the government not promoting a new kind of *caveat emptor?*

If the consumer is truly to be protected—from the confusion of legalism as well as from the confusion of technology—business and institutional management must lead the way. They are close to the marketplace and have perfected the communications skills well enough for them to cooperate with government in doing a better job of informing the consumer. Good managers will find better ways to communicate if they really believe in the consumer. And I think they do.   [1973]

46   *Regulation and Deregulation: A Dialog*

There are those who contend that *any* discussion of deregulation is unnecessary; they favor just getting rid of the to them obviously unnecessary regulations. But I do not know of any regulation the formulation of which did not involve very long discussions. Certainly, then, any move toward deregulation deserves as much—or more—consideration. Healthy discussion is a quest for wisdom.

Discussion of regulation also highlights that some regulation is part of every society, and a complex society will have complex regulations. Discussion will also help us to uncover the regulations that all of us believe can be improved. Further, it should help us dissipate some of the suspicions that affect the attitudes of those in business, in government, or in public interest groups; this alone should advance understanding and perhaps lead to a constructive modification of existing regulations—or reactions to them.

DISCUSSION ENLIGHTENS

Discussion will also show that there is no *one* business point of view; the very nature of competition gets in the way of a common point of view. Oh, sometimes business people find common cause, but not on major issues.

Most people in business are hard working and enjoy being good citizens. They react humanly to the subtle entrapment of some regulations, particularly when the regulator appears to be more interested in headlines than in conformity with the law.

Actually, this powerful economic force called business is afraid. The proprietary nature of entrepreneurship, the secretive aspects of competition, the perception of responsibility for others' assets, and a healthy personal ambition combine into an attitude that leads businessmen and -women to resist efforts to control their activities. To them, regulations are threats.

UNINTENDED EFFECTS

It is unfortunate, too, that laws that may have a good social purpose are sometimes framed in such a way as to raise questions about the knowledge and insight of legislators and/or government agents into the nature of modern business. OSHA is a case in point. There is a sincere social purpose involved. But the law is written in a way that raises serious questions about the secondary effects of its enforcement in industry. For example, the trend in management over the past 20 years has been toward decentralization. But OSHA's approach is predicated on an authoritarian organizational philosophy, a philosophy that is absolutely dead in progressive companies. If I as president of a company can go to jail for a violation of OSHA regulations in my company, how much freedom of action do you think I will delegate to others? Very little! The result? A new spate of regulation to correct the damage to worker satisfaction attributable to the lessened delegation.

For most laws and regulations, the government worker charged with implementing or enforcing them usually played little part in making them, and therefore may not fully understand their purposes. But most do their best. Among the millions of government workers, though, there are bound to be some who consider the businessman or -woman as an adversary. These are misfits, and conscientious administrators must help them correct that attitude—or replace them. In any case, good government workers—and there are many—*must* be dedicated since there are so few extrinsic rewards for above-average performance.

DEMOCRACY IS US

All who are seriously concerned with the economic warp and woof of our society agree that business and government must serve the public interest. The public interest, however, will be defined differently by consumer groups, unions, universities, and other groups. Each group is made up of diverse human beings, and every personality and taste is involved. *We* dealing with *us* is not easy. Self-dealing always causes problems. As consumers we all wonder how to get to big government and big business. Just this last week, for example, I wanted to march on my building superintendent, the traffic department, New York taxi drivers, and dog owners—and this was a good week. And I did find that talking to some of them helped wonderfully.

Discussion—of regulation, deregulation, or any other subject—does work. It is democracy at work, and it works because it is *us*.   [1977]

47   Social Responsibility—An Ounce of Anticipation . . .

One smokestack is development. Two smokestacks is competition. Three smokestacks is pollution.

At a recent meeting of managers from around the world, I was impressed by the broadly shared concern among managers from developed countries over the third smokestack—and similar matters bearing on their social responsibility. I was also impressed by the attitude of those from the developing countries who would happily settle for the first smokestack. (And then there were managers from those countries who were concerned only with the second smokestack represented by multinational companies operating on their soil.)

The managers concerned about pollution *wanted* to do something about it. At the same time, they were perplexed. Where had the problem come from—so suddenly? "I can remember," one manager said, "when the smoke coming out of our stack made everyone in town feel optimistic. . .they saw it as a signal that business was good. How come I'm suddenly a villain?"

A TRANSFORMATION

Town heros had become town villains—almost overnight—because of the "marginal smokestack." Community growth had resulted in so many smokestacks that, suddenly, what had been a welcome single smokestack became an unacceptable belching "three stacks" and a pervasive social problem drawing fire from almost every quarter. We can see *now* that this problem could have been anticipated.

Anticipating changes in social needs and concerns is becoming increasingly important in the management of any corporation. But

153

this is more easily said than done. One place to start is to look at history. What problems have already occurred? What were their antecedents? How had the company reacted?

Next, a social audit provides a productive approach to assessing the nature and adequacy of a company's response to current demands for socially responsible behavior. But a social audit is not very precise and concentrates on where an organization is now. Audits are of little use in projecting where the organization is headed; they must be supplemented by speculations and projections of trends based on external data.

USING A CLOUDY CRYSTAL BALL

Looking to the future always involves a cloudy crystal ball. But not attempting to foresee the future entails unacceptable risks—as the dazed manager discovered when the community reacted to the marginal smokestack.

Despite the risk inherent in forecasting, then, today's manager must make judgments concerning future areas of social concern. But how? To begin with, he must stay alert to the way that others, outside the organization, perceive the society evolving. And managers must remember that many perceptions and projections of forthcoming social problems become self-fulfilling prophecies. Present legislative and regulatory trends, for example, have developed from concern over equal rights for women and others, product safety, conservation of natural resources, and ways of bringing minority groups into the economic mainstream—as workers and as consumers.

SPOTTING TRENDS IN THE MAKING

What trends *are* in the making that will probably lead to tomorrow's issues? One is growth in the proportion of old people versus young people in our society—a ratio that will grow even larger with continuing improvements in medical care. What could this increase mean for corporate retirement policies? Pensions? Social Security?

Medicare? Most companies' approach to retiring employees is elementary at present—it will have to change. For example, companies in the future will in all likelihood be making a more concerted effort to use the still viable talents of retirees than they are at present. Isn't it reasonable, too, to foresee more widely available low-cost housing designed for retirees? And why not certain kinds of plants and offices in these communities to provide productive, meaningful work for those who wish it?

Spotting and projecting social movements require today's manager to be open enough and flexible enough to consider currently remote possibilities. Done well, this will help companies to respond in a timely and positive manner to new social demands.   [1975]

48   *Society's Right to Jobs*

Not having a job imposes a stigma that is unacceptable to most people. Those with feelings of personal worth want to utilize their talents productively, support their families, participate in a few luxuries of life.

In industrialized societies, a job is a basic element in this drive for self-sufficiency; and for those who prize this status, particularly in difficult economies where job opportunities are limited, the earnings of a job are basic to personal freedom. For an increasing number of people, then, a job has become the most significant property right of our time.

Ensuring this right imposes a heavy responsibility on all society. When approached on the question of their role, traditional managers tend to respond by pointing out that they do indeed furnish jobs and contribute mightily to government programs to relieve unemployment. True enough, but is it not possible that this reply is too "traditional"? Do traditional motivations for furnishing jobs now meet the test of our times? Can we rest comfortably on the assumption that job-seekers should conform precisely to specific needs? To what extent can we continue to tailor job requirements only to total salary levels that assure a profit?

NEED FOR NEW ANSWERS

The right to a job and the social disposition to support those who cannot exercise this right will call for much new management thinking before this century is out. If the private sector does not generate productive ideas, governments will continue to mandate job programs and allocate taxes accordingly. Can managers really afford to pass up opportunities for leadership on the issue of employment and thereby accept bureaucracy as the way to balance the economy and the rights of individuals? More and more the right to a job is forcing new answers on managers and unions.

Job design practices provide a case in point. In an industrialized society with an engineering approach to the division of labor, job specialization remains important to our operational routine. We are still comfortable with the heritage of the technical school, the secretarial college, the schools of accounting, and other specializations that for years prepared carefully selected students for functional careers—and easily placed their graduates in jobs. Pace Institute, Carnegie Tech, Drexel, Katherine Gibbs are just a few of the great names among the institutions that served a burgeoning job market with superbly trained specialists. But the notion, born in the Industrial Revolution, that one person be assigned one specialized task appears to be yielding to innovations in job design. Traditional approaches to the ways we specify and slot specific jobs are changing fast.

TECHNOLOGY VERSUS EDUCATION

But are we moving fast enough? We have gaps at many levels in our scale of job needs. Today, for example, technology tends to outrun education. Newly acquired degrees foster great expectations among graduates, but only a few are ready to team up with robots, computers, and satellites when they report to employers and begin to accept their first post-graduation pay checks. With the drudgery of many jobs now being turned over to mechanical and electronic devices that labor as well as, or perhaps even better than, human workers, our needs demand even higher talent for thinking, creating, inventing, controlling, and developing.

While responding to this call for educational refocusing, the private sector must also attend to social responsibilities elsewhere—such as funneling more jobs to the employable elderly, to minorities, to the less talented. A reduction in minimum wages and an awakening of unions to responsibilities beyond the immediate needs of their members would open many possibilities not attainable under present unreal restrictions on total use of the available workforce.

The direction, if not the precise pattern, of pending changes can be detected abroad. For reasons quite different from those bearing on U.S. industry, companies in other countries are trying forms of organization that our theorists have been advocating for years. In Europe, worker participation in management and in shop-floor decision making, for example, has been widely accepted—though under legislative mandate; each country where it has been institutionalized, however, uses it in varying degrees and in widely differentiated formats. In Japan, the Japanese tradition of lifetime employment has given many companies unusual opportunities to meet specific social and economic needs.

None of these formulas is working perfectly, and none stands out as necessarily right for the United States. But they do suggest the direction of our ultimate destination in the matter of jobs planning.

WORKING AS A GROUP

The group concept provides another case in point. Formulas for job description, standards of performance, individual performance evaluation, and merit rewards are undergoing modification to accommodate an accelerating shift into group activity and related participatory modes of on-the-job operations.

Although we may not say goodbye entirely to individual job specifications, groups will eventually be the basic work unit. In the one-job/one-person concept, individual qualification is basic; success and satisfaction are linked to the specific job. Not all people are created with the same or equal talent, however, and fewer develop their talents in the same way. Groups accommodate this diversity by accepting a variety of talents, including lesser abilities. Success and satisfaction thus become linked to overall group performance, not individual success.

The intense competition so often generated under our present-day one-job/one-person formula can lead to politics on the job, cause many difficult interpersonal problems, lower productivity, and create endless compensation dilemmas. Such competition can also be beneficial, of course, but normally must be carefully directed and monitored closely for best results.

Groups, on the other hand, spark the magic of creative thinking at all levels. Research teams, for example, have long been a part of laboratory operations. Task forces are widely used to tackle major problems requiring special solutions.

In its refined form, the group permits the private sector to seek, instead of just accepting, those of limited ability. A manager ordinarily takes a risk when hiring a person with limited talent. But in a group design, the same person can be put to work productively with no risk of "overemployment."

In baseball, the bat boy and the designated hitter both serve limited roles, but are proud of their team and share in its rewards. In the industrial workplace, a janitor can become part of Team A, not because sweeping the floor is necessarily a vital job, but a clear work area is important, and the sweeper contributes to his fellow workers' sense of team achievement.

Hiring into groups thus will be necessarily quite different from hiring for individual work-alone or assembly-line jobs. All members will be in on the selection—and on the rejection as well when members decide it is necessary to squeeze out a reluctant performer.

PRIVATE-SECTOR LEADERSHIP

What's really important in this scope of change is the opportunity offered to the private sector to shift its notion of isolation in social development and begin to lead social thinking. Managers who took the first step toward bringing women and minorities into the workforce are easily capable of designing a system that will use all able-bodied individuals.

The basic challenge is finding the source of economic leadership. I think it lies in the private sector—where it should be.   [1981]

49   *This Is the Year*

We in the United States are rich beneficiaries of our economic system, a system that may be described as entrepreneurial, competitive, capitalistic, or all of these. Managers in this system have combined risk taking, competition, and private ownership of the means of production and distribution within a climate of freedom. As we approach our two-hundredth anniversary, however, it might be well for managers in business and industry to examine what is happening to the system that has made our society the most imitated one yet to exist.

Today, everyone seems to have *something* to say about our economic system, usually critical. Opponents of the system make the headlines. Some firmly oppose it, believing goverment can solve all problems, even if the result must be complete government control. A few, in protecting their own little "pea patch"—be it an industry or a labor union—cannot be bothered with anything as elusive as "a system." And always there are those who just cannot be bothered with *anything*.

MANAGERS AND THE SYSTEM

As we enter the year that started July 4, 1975, managers who would preserve the system are in disarray. As a consequence, they have approached their self-chosen task in a manner very unlike that of professional managers and have, as a group, failed on practically every count in their attempts to defend and preserve free enterprise: Their efforts have been described as being as "effective as changing deck chairs on the Titanic."

Free enterprise has always been dynamic. In the past, though, changes came primarily from within the system. A brief study of the evolution of business institutions, for instance, will show dynamic internal changes as the units of the system moved from individual proprietorships through various forms of partnerships to take the form of the modern corporation. (The form of establishments changed because personal liability and capital limitations were too restrictive in their ability to grow rapidly enough to serve expanding needs.) The managers of these institutions had freedom to decide and to move, and they moved in innovative ways.

ADAM SMITH'S WISDOM

Today, with change being forced on businesses from the outside, managers are tending to adopt an attitude much like Adam Smith's when he wrote, "I have never known much good done by those who affected to trade for the public good." Most managers would like to return to Smith's "obvious and simple system of natural liberty." But pressures and constraints from the outside are not going to go away easily.

In the past, the opportunity for managerial self-sufficiency inspired in managers the verve of rugged individualism. Basically, freedom is never far from individualism, and good management stresses individualism. A constant challenge of management has been the reconciliation of the free spirit of the individual with the desire many individuals have to accomplish more by being members of a team. But now, if we are to solve the problems of our free enterprise system, we will *need* to come together in a collective and coordinated effort.

COMPETITION VERSUS COOPERATION

There is no question but that competition has produced substantial benefits for our customers and our country. But competition in providing products and services should not carry over to lack of cooperation in defending the system that is so important to us all. Some have said that the bickering among us would bring our house down if it were not for our common need to oppose our *external* critics and antagonists. But need this be so? Might we not more appropriately come together under a neutral sponsor, not in reaction against external dangers, but to develop joint plans to advance the principles of our system?

To properly identify our problem and plan for its alleviation require that we marshal our top talent, forget our "old-boys club," stop throwing money at mediocre solutions, and work together to preserve a *good* system—the best that has been developed so far.   [1975]